We Have
the Kind of
God Who Gives

WE HAVE
THE KIND OF
GOD WHO GIVES

THE GIVING POWER OF GOD

DENNIS FRAZIER

authorHOUSE®

AuthorHouse™
1663 Liberty Drive
Bloomington, IN 47403
www.authorhouse.com
Phone: 1 (800) 839-8640

Published by AuthorHouse 03/23/2016

ISBN: 978-1-5049-4867-8 (sc)
ISBN: 978-1-5049-4866-1 (e)

TABLE OF CONTENTS

THE BEST FOR YOU IS EVER SO PRESENT!

"We are not here by accident or mistake we all have a specific purpose given by God."

In this book I go back in my child-hood which brings out the good and bad experiences that led me into a successful walk with God. Also to encourage the person or persons who feel that where they are at this point of their life is their final destination. I explain that we determine our destination and also we determine when our life is ended.

When the actual truth is, there is marvelous and productive potential in all of us. This sleepy giant of success has to wake up and take control of our life before tragedy and misfortunes destroy us.

As you read this material, you will experience a positive shift in your life and that's the giant awakening and he's starting to propel you into your true passion in the things of God. Once we realize our true identity that within itself will ignite zeal to diligently seek our destiny. Our greatness will be a common pattern of our thought life. Success after success will be our daily accomplishment and knowing that we are a treasure to each other.

By Dennis Frazier, Author

CREDITS

To my Parents, Albert and Verience Frazier; Daddy, You have paved a Godly path for Your Family which has developed us into Women and Men of God that only promotes Righteousness. Mom, Your tender and gentle Hand of Love has directed This Family into being Strong Soldiers of Truth, which defeats darkness. Thank You!

To my only Daughter,

I dearly love You, there's not a day that goes by when I don't think of You. You will always remain a large portion of my "Joy." May God continue to keep You safe in His Peace so that You may walk in His Blessings Daily. Amen!

To my only Son,

I'm so proud of Your musical gift and how God has developed You into a strong and fine Man of God. I Love You! May You also continue to Walk in God's Blessings Daily! I constantly pray for the both of You! Amen!

My Spiritual Father and Mother, Pastor Thomas and Annette Riley, You passionately Teach God's People Love, Truth, and Integrity. Countless times You have prepared platforms of Righteousness for us to follow. Also, You have awaken in me an Awesome God Awareness and created an appetite for my spirit man to become "The Giant" in my life. Thank You!

PREFACE

There are times in life where we may be in an undesirable situation caused by some of the decisions we made. We may think that we have no way out just like I thought at one time. We may find ourselves searching for relief or answers that will remove us from this misery.

Often times we choose methods that we have been accustomed to because of influential figures that were just as stuck as we or possible peer pressure who make our decisions for us. After going through long periods or even years of useless efforts and wasted energy of using what we thought was going to be our way out. We ended up digging ourselves into a deeper pit of havoc and chaos.

As in the case of some of us, we felt we had all the answers regardless of what kind of truth that was working against us. Our pride became a silent killer and that led us into a spiraling ignorance that only rewarded us one failure after another.

It's a shame some of us had to choose this road of hard knocks to come to our God given senses. To only realize that we were designed to dominate our earthly ruler ship which grants us victories, triumphs, and accomplishments.

This book gives hope through God's Promises and how receiving His Promises is a redemptive right that we are entitled to through The Blood of Jesus.

I share my weaknesses and my strengths, also how my strengths over came my weaknesses and led me to an Awesome God Awareness that never ends and gets more exciting, by breaking barriers, with every encounter.

I encourage people that you don't have to remain in your present situation only if you choose to grab hold of God's Word and allow His Word to change your mindsets. For His Word to remove the strong holds that defeat us on a daily basis.

I explain how the application of God's Word can benefit any situation in any walk of life no matter what age group or ethnic background. God's Word does not discriminate; His Word will work for anyone who will get involved.

Like David said in Psalms 34:8, "O taste and see that The Lord is good."

This book is loaded with sweet encounters from my childhood to this present point and time in my life. And the good part about this is that these encounters continue on. Because I also understand even some of my dark days had their place in my bright development. When we mess up I believe sometimes God scratches His head and says, "Ok I forgive you, go ahead and get up and start again because we got work to do."

This book is very personal to me because I broke through some personal barriers; eliminated some strongholds; and allowed some of what God had put in me to surface into my true identity.

As I share my life's experiences you may relate to them or you may not but, one thing for sure you will see and understand how The Hand of God can bring everything out for our good.

My only objective is to encourage someone to come up to their full Godly potential and to realize that where you are is not your final destination.

There is so much value still in you, also unlimited potentials, and attaining goals never before imagined. Only if we step out of the box of negative thinking and acquire and operate in God's Kingdom Principles by being what His Word says we are.

It's not too late, as long as you have breath in your body and willingness to better yourself then this can happen. And if the truth be told, we are not too far out there where God is not able to bring us back. I may not be the only success story that many of you have heard. God wants us to reach out with our success stories that will give people hope and direction.

We being in "The Body of Christ" we collectively have an impact to make for God and individually we have a mission to fulfill. There is plenty of room at the top and the top is where we were designed to be.

I also go in detail of the necessary steps we all have taken or need to take to fulfill our God given purpose and walk in the destiny He has planned for each of our lives.

Along with understanding that our natural birth, into this earth, was not a mistake and our existence is highly valuable and to believe that we are the most important being in this universe. God brought us here to do a designed work although different assignments but all for the same cause, which is promoting, "The Gospel of the Kingdom," simply put, our work is an extension of what Jesus did.

Another important fact is that, before the foundations of the world began God knew I would be writing this and that you would be reading it. It doesn't matter where you are in life right now, I am sure that I mention you somewhere in this material. So allow this experience to be a process of renewal as you enter into your levels of awareness.

You Are So Blessed and Loved by God and His Family, The Church!

Dennis Frazier, Author
Dennisfrazier58@yahoo.com

CHAPTER 1

GOD GIVES US HIS WORD FOR US TO OVERCOME

Everything God gives or does is for Love because God is Love. God cannot do anything without first exhibiting The Spirit of Giving that's all Love knows is The Spirit if Giving. Because Love knows that giving always benefits the party who is to receive it. It's impossible for Him to operate outside of the realm of who He is, which is Love. God will never get tired of giving nor will He ever run out of things to give just as long as we are willing to receive we will have His Best one hundred percent of the time.

We see in John 3:16 "God so Loved the world He gave." Well, what did He give? Simple, He gave Himself through the Virgin Mary by way of Jesus Christ, The Anointed One. Why? Because, God knew nothing could or has out lasted Him. He's everlasting and everything, all that He does is everlasting. There's no end to God; He's eternal; His plan has no expiration date; doesn't get stale; neither is His Plan confusing. God's plan has been the same for thousands of years already and will cover all through eternity.

You see, Family, the Awesomeness of God cannot be measured through our human thinking or our physical knowledge, knowing Him is all spiritual. In Isaiah 55:9 God says, "My ways are higher than your ways, My thoughts than your thoughts." In Revelation 1:8 says, "I am Alpha and Omega, the beginning and the ending..."

This also tells us if He is the beginning and the ending then He also knows, or is, everything between those two points. Jeremiah 32:27 says, "I am the Lord, The God of all flesh:" (simply put that all flesh has came out of Him) [The Giver and Creator of Life].

Again in Jeremiah 1:5 states, "Before I formed thee in the belly I knew thee; and before thou comest out of the womb I sanctified thee, and I ordained thee a prophet unto the nations." So God originated our spirit

1

man in Heaven first then He sent our spirit into the earth by way of natural birth, just like Jesus.

Philippians 3:20 (AMP) "But we are citizens of the state (commonwealth, homeland) which is in Heaven." Our identity and true citizenship is in Heaven and those of us who are in the body of Christ and when our spirit leaves our body by natural death then we'll return back to our homeland, which is in Heaven. II Corinthians 5:8 …"to be absent from the body, and to be present with the Lord."

We are not here by accident or mistake we all have a specific purposes given by God. The only way we can come to know the Mind of God or fulfilling His purpose is Faith and obedience in His Word. It all starts with a quality decision in making Jesus our personal Saviour. Being born again is accepting The Salvation process which is a condition of our heart by repentance and faith in The Lord Jesus. Repentance opens the heart to turn from self-efforts to having faith in God, His faith that we now believe in now clears the way of all lies and rationalizing or compromising against His Truth. Repentance simply means to turn away from wickedness (wrong doing) to a state of belief and acceptance in a relationship with Jesus Christ. Once we make that all important decision then we are to rely on Him for everything and He is more than able to supply us with all that we may ever need or want.

This is the only way that we can be delivered from the bondage of sins curses and receives wholeness in spirit, soul, and body. The only effort on our part for accepting Jesus Christ as our personal Saviour is belief by saying, "That if thou shalt confess with thy mouth the Lord Jesus, and shalt believe in thine heart that God hath raised Him from the dead, thou shalt be saved. Romans 10:9 Just quoting that verse with our heart full of belief is enough to guarantee full acceptance into The Family of God also, this is where our faith begins, "the just shall live by faith" Galatians 3:11 and "but without faith it is impossible to please Him (God)" Hebrews 11:6. Faith is a confidence, and, belief in God which cannot be measured by our human senses, however, trust that His Word is real and that His Word will do exactly what His Word says. God speaks of what His Word will do in Isaiah 55:11 "So shall My Word that goeth forth out of my mouth: it shall not return unto Me void, but it shall accomplish that which I please, and it shall prosper in the thing whereto I sent it." So is the same effect when we speak God's Word into situations.

Now that you have made Romans 10:9 a part of your life, this is the first step to increase your faith in The Word of God. And this step gives God total access and entrance into our lives, which is extremely necessary. This is the most important decision a person can ever make no matter what the age. And since we have made a decision to live and not die now we can make better decisions pertaining to "The Good Life" in "Christ Jesus."

There's something else that takes place when we receive God into our lives, we automatically become The Righteousness of God. Simply put we are now in right standing with Him and we now can approach Him without shame, guilt, or condemnation. Hebrews 4:16 states, "Let us therefore come boldly unto the Throne of Grace, that we may obtain Mercy, and find Grace to help in time of need." Romans 10:10, "For with the heart man believeth unto righteousness; and with the mouth confession is made unto salvation."

By us covering those two areas, believing that The Lord Jesus was raised to redeem us from the curse of sin and we have also confessed this belief with our mouths. Now The Righteousness of God is in operation in our lives and there's a certain boldness that comes with our Righteousness. Proverbs 28:1, "but the righteous are bold as a lion." This boldness allows us to step out on our faith and demand the results that God's Word says we can have. Boldly confessing God's Word and believing what we are confessing will happen always gets God's attention with results every time.

In Mark 11:24 Jesus is speaking, "Therefore I say unto you, What things soever ye desire, when ye pray, believe that ye receive them, and ye shall have them." A perfect example of how we should receive God's Promises, Jesus spoke this with complete understanding.

Every institution or establishment in life has standards or principles that must be followed. For instance the military, our law enforcement, our schools, our hospitals, and of course our jobs just to name a few. Now we follow those standards so we can receive the benefit from that particular system that we are involved in. And if the truth be told, life's principles and values first came out God by way of Adam and Eve.

In The Kingdom of God, He has set-up principles and guidelines that must be obeyed. It seems we have no problem doing what our job requires or what a financial institution demands of us, and we understand that compromising their principles is not an option. The fact is where we place most or all of our confidence in will determine where our benefits come from.

God *Gives* His Plan of Life for our benefit He only wants entrance into our lives. This is the only way His Spiritual Presence can give physical manifestations in our lives daily.

Faith in His Word is a necessity for us to have a focused walk and keeping our confidence on and receiving His Promises. God has equipped us with everything we need to live in this life and even more things we have when we live for Him. Let's face it Family, we already have The God kind of Faith, "He dealt to every man the measure of faith Romans 12:3."

Accepting God into our lives quickens our faith and makes our faith to become alive. When our faith comes alive, our faith start to beckon for The Holy Spirit and The Holy Spirit wants to lovingly become part of our lives and continue to reside in our physical bodies having total liberty to function in all areas of our lives. God did not design us to live any other way 1Corinthians 6:19-20 (AMP), "Do you know that your body is the temple (the very sanctuary) of The Holy Spirit Who lives within you, Whom you have received [as a Gift] from God? You are not your own,

You (we) were bought with a price [purchased with a preciousness and paid for, made His own], So then, honor God and bring glory to Him in your body."

How beautiful and exciting to know that I can have The Holy Spirit operating in me and through me by Him leading me and guiding me in all "Truth" directing my steps; giving me understanding; revealing my purpose; and comforting me through difficult times. To receive The

Precious Gift of The Holy Spirit all a person has to do is raise their hands to The Heavens and with praise and thanksgiving ask The Holy Spirit to come up on you. And you will begin to speak the language of The Holy Spirit. You can repeat this process as many times as necessary until you have allowed The Holy Spirit to come up on you. In The Book of Acts chapter one and verse eight in The Amplified Version Jesus says, "But ye shall receive power (ability, efficiency, and might) when The Holy Spirit has come upon you," sounds like to me The Holy Spirit is a one man army with all the Host of Heaven operating on the inside of us.

The more earnest we become during this process the more effective this process becomes and all of Heaven is praising and rejoicing right along with us. And it's nothing wrong if you want to enjoy this moment for hours or even days because this is a new experience an eternal experience. You've just invited A Holy Army into your life and to allow their forces to operate on a daily basis for us. A new birth has just taken place, the ultimate in an earthly experience nothing can or has compared to this eternal and massive experience. I've seen people who have allowed The Holy Spirit come upon them and they act as if nothing happen. This is the type of person doesn't understand what just took place in their life.

Just like when a new born baby enters into this world their cry is proof that there is life. The same scenario when The Holy Spirit comes upon us our rejoicing is proof that the life of The Holy Spirit is present. The Holy Spirit always brings rejoicing, maybe tears of joy which is evidence that we have allowed The Peace of God to enter into our life. Our understanding determines our expression rather it be rejoicing or just a casual walk back to our seat. Something so awesome as having God Almighty operate in our lives is not just a casual experience.

This is the first of many times Heaven now smiles at us and all the people who are in Heaven that we know is probably doing back flips because of us allowing The Holy Spirit to come upon us. They might be looking over at The Throne of God and say, "Thank You Lord!" Heaven doesn't mind at all rejoicing on our behalf Isaiah 62:5 (AMP), "and as the bridegroom rejoices over the bride, so shall your God rejoice over you." Please understand that God always rejoices over the triumphs that He has brought us through.

III John :4, "I have no greater joy than to hear that my children walk in truth." If God places high priority over our life's accomplishments, through His Word, then we should share with Him in that same joy.

Allowing the Gift of The Holy Spirit to operate in our lives is a feeling that cannot be compared to any other feeling on earth. Such a feeling of peace it seems like tears of joy will not end and actually the joy won't stop as long as we continue this practice daily. Just like we practice or participate in our natural meals to nourish our physical bodies the same principle applies to our "spirit man."

Of course we won't need to be filled with The Holy Spirit daily however we need to practice the presence of The Holy Spirit daily and each time is never like the last it just gets better each time we practice His presence. During this time of fellowship with The Father is when we get more of His Peace, His Answers, and our direction becomes clearer this is just part of His daily benefits that He gives to us.

Please understand that I mention these processes of accepting Christ in your life and receiving The Holy Spirit in the event that you may not know where a Word based Church is located where teaching The Truth with passion is demonstrated. And we all need to be in a Word teaching Church that enforces The Truth. Jeremiah 3:15 reads, "And I will give Pastors according to Mine Heart, which shall feed you with knowledge and understanding." So allow the pure leading of The Holy Spirit in your quest that is if you are not already established in a Church Family and receiving The Truth. Simply put, it is the choice of The Father where we need to be and be taught The Truth of God's Word. In this type of obedience is where our purpose will be developed because of the vision God has placed in this Pastor and through this vision is when our development for our purpose will manifest. How can we teach if we don't first be taught?

What I'm sharing with you in this book comes from about ten to twelve years of earnest teachings and me applying what my Man of God is showing us in The Word of God.

Because what I'm about to share with you in the upcoming chapters it will take The Holy Spirit to give you full understanding. And if you don't understand the first time then be at liberty to go over this material as often as possible. I just want people to take their time going through this book. I bring out some strong points about my life some of which I don't want people to make the same mistake. And other parts I just want you to rejoice with me in my triumphs.

Now, that we have made the decision to make Jesus your personal Saviour, and have ushered in The Holy Spirit into your life and we understand that we have faith. Now where do we go from here? This is the time to begin to develop our mind into thinking like an overcomer and start living in our Royal Priesthood.

1 Peter 2:9 explains, "But ye are a chosen generation, a royal priesthood, an holy nation, a peculiar people; that ye should show forth the praises of Him who hath called you out of darkness into His marvellous light:"

Now we understand that nothing or no one can penetrate our "spirit man" because we are reading, studying, and confessing God's Word into our lives daily. This practice directs our thinking to line-up with what The Bible is saying and we live in daily expectation for this gradual change to take place. This is also an indication our faith is growing because we must work this muscle of faith to unlimited potentials. Romans 10:17 So then faith *cometh* by hearing, and hearing by the Word of God.

The more we hear God's Word and the more we learn how to apply His Word in our daily living the stronger our faith gets. Then we'll begin to experience Godly Manifestations over and over on a regular basis.

When we take this life that He gave us intertwined this life with the Faith He gave us we get the results that He wants us to have. Now, God is proud of us because living for Him allows us to lay up eternal treasures for what we do down here on earth and we also receive His rewards here on earth. So, I ask what we are doing with the faith that God has dealt to each and every one of us and how can we make Him proud? We are equipped with every essential tool to prosper with the faith God has given to us.

I'm sure a lot of this most of you already know, and that's good. My only purpose is to bring understanding for someone to get to the fullness of what God has done in my life and what His Word says who He is, and how we can better apply His Word in our daily living. By doing that, you will begin to experience triumphs never before thought possible and need I mention also receiving an abundance of God's Promises before we get to Heaven. Amen?

CHAPTER 2

GOD GIVES US HIS DELIVERANCE

I have found such an "excitement" in living for The Father which keeps me inspired through His "Joy;" keeps me focused through His "Peace;" and "His Word" keeps me seeking for more ways of how He can become "more real" in my life. God has already delivered me from drugs; homelessness; joblessness; and the agony of mental defeat.

I first got introduced to alcohol and smoking cigarettes in my early teenage years approximately age nine or ten. You have to understand back in those days certain things a person did was more trustworthy. What I mean is that children could buy cigarettes and alcohol as long as we had a note from our parents. I always hung out with the older crowd so getting that kind of note was not a problem. I guess one might say "I'm one of the reasons that have changed over the years." Of course, to where now there are age limits on purchasing cigarettes and alcohol.

How good would it be to raise a generation who hasn't seen a beer commercial? Or a television program where alcohol isn't used. They always show fine upstanding and successful people participating in alcohol consummation. Instead of promoting the dangers of this "liquid drug." And how it destroys our internal organs and makes our dependency uncontrollable even into possible death.

When we see medicine introduce on the market the side effects is always stated. Our foods are always labeled with what is in them. Then it's up to us rather we want to take this chance of using this product and suffer the consequences. Shouldn't we be given the same choice when it comes to alcohol consummation? Even on packs of cigarettes it states the physical risk that's involved from using those products.

I remember prices in our economy were not shooting through the roof. I remember cigarettes use to be twenty six cents; the lowest gas prices I can remember were thirty eight cents per gallon; bread was priced at twenty six cents.

I learned that most children on my age level were doing the normal things such as being a child and getting an education and allowing their lives and bodies to develop in a healthy way. At that time healthy living would seem boring, and little did I know doing drugs, alcohol, and cigarettes at my age could effect my physical and mental development and maybe lead into an early death.

There was a huge void present in my life that I was not aware of, and I tried to fill it by doing the wrong thing. Hiding this from my parents and relatives was also stressful and I found myself lying over and over again.

There were many times as a child I would envy or feel out of place with the children who were doing the right thing. This was the time where I developed a strong inferior complex with myself; you see one of the characteristics if sin is to rob you of your true identity through guilt, shame, and condemnation. The attitude that sin gave taught me to cheat, lie and even steal from my parents. Thank God, I never took these horrible characteristics outside of the home. I never stole in the public where Law Enforcement would have handled me through the judicial system, I was terrified of jail.

No one knew at the time what was happening, or so I thought, and neither did I know how serious my situation was. But one thing for sure, if not dealt with properly it would plague me my whole life.

Even though my parents were the ideal parents, for me, when it came to loving us and providing the necessities of the home I still thought I was smarter and began to develop my own agenda of what life was suppose to be. Little did I know that I had been deceived into my own self centeredness with defeat as my only reward.

I began to develop the idea that good things or the better way of living were for other people. How could I qualify for these good things when at such an early age I started to acquire "grown folks" baggage? Again, guilt, shame, and condemnation had me thinking I could never measure up.

In school I did enough just to get by and never applied myself to excel past average or most times being satisfied with being below average. The only reason why I didn't make many failing grades was because my Mom and Dad strongly enforced discipline by way of the belt, Thank God for their discipline.

Learning higher academics were for the other children or so I thought. I believed it was a trick to learning and since I didn't qualify for that trick I was satisfied with my present condition and developed a bad trait where I would start something and not finish it.

This type of lifestyle continued until I became a freshman in high school. Then seem like God must've said enough was enough because He began to lead me into His direction by way of my parents. I started to develop a strong attraction for church and church activities. Singing in the choir, playing some musical instruments, and was on the usher board.

Having the Holy Ghost became something that I wanted, and of course needed. I was fifteen years old (December fifteenth nineteen sixty eight) when I ask the Holy Spirit to come up on my life. I remember this marvelous event like it was yesterday. I couldn't sleep at all that night because of the excitement; I was either laughing or crying from the joy that I was experiencing. It was like a high that just got better and better.

I acquired a love for reading The Bible and I always wanted to go to church even if I had to walk. I remember sitting on the church steps waiting for someone to come and open up.

I loved walking through the sanctuary; the fresh and clean smell that was always there; the shinny polished wooden support beams that would glow just from the smallest glimmer of light. The sound or the organ and piano during service times was so uplifting; the songs we would sing would keep ringing in my ears from service to service. As you can see, I became sensitive to the simple or small things and noticed how beautiful they were.

All I seen in the church members was their sincerity and devotion to God, also to our Pastor, and to the church. So many times I would gleam from that sincerity and devotion and I began to grow into a man of God. How could I not want to be a part of God's ordained family, I finally got a taste of heaven right here on earth at an early age.

Now I could allow myself to become one of those children that focused in on healthy living and take my school academics more seriously. My grades began to improve because I had realize how important study time was for learning and also preparing for tests I never was held back or failed any of my grades, regardless of my earlier years when I had a strong lack of interest in my academics.

Or maybe having a Dad who was six feet four inches tall and weighing two hundred sixty pounds with no pot belly and no flab had something to do with me not failing in school. Daddy could run a full sprint in his fifty's and sixty's only if he would have played professional sports. But if he did maybe he would not have had the opportunity to directly instill in me some of life's truest values.

And because of his fatherhood directing my manhood for me he was the perfect father and Man of God. He may not have been famous throughout the world however besides God he was the most famous Man I've ever known. To list the many ways My Dad had a positive effect on me would be in a book by itself and maybe name the book My Dad. Hmm?

My Dad went home to be with The Lord in December of two thousand and for the impact he had on my life sometimes it seems he's still here. I can still hear his voice coaching me through tough times and telling me how proud he is of my accomplishments. Also he affirmed me, in his few last days, that I would be a better man than him. Wow, what an awesome achievement and one of the ways to become better is to take what he taught me to higher levels by applying Godly Principles. Those are some pretty big shoes to fill, but with The Anointing of God on my life, I'm ready for the challenge one step at a time.

CHAPTER 3

GOD GIVES US HIS PATH FOR US TO WALK IN

In elementary school playing football was a strong love for me. Now that I was in high school I had to learn the balance between football and church activities, however through God's Wisdom teaching me how to prioritize. I was able to keep my grades up, attend church and keep reading my bible and play football.

When playing football I always kept a starting position year after year I easily developed a technique for the game. Track was also my strong point I thoroughly enjoyed the relay teams, sports gave me discipline as far as following instructions and keeping a strong positive attitude for winning. I found myself taking it to the next level mostly because the coach's seen my sincerity and would show me the best way to utilize my skills and be more productive.

Plus I had the favor of God on my side in such a way whenever other players would make mistakes they would have to do extra exercises. But if I made a mistake I would be told the correct way to do something plus the coaches would tell other players do it like Frazier.

I developed the mindset of what it meant to have team work and how to depend on your teammates and how they could depend on you. For those of you who understand football positions I played left defensive end.

When I was in elementary school I decided to play this position because I didn't like being hit but, of course, I liked doing the hitting. Playing defense gave you the legal right to dish out some athletic punishment. It seemed that football was made specifically for me. In my junior year I was recognized as being all-city now to me that was an honor for doing the little that I did. However having said all that, my junior year in high school was the end of my short career of football.

To this day I still love the game, of course, by following my favorite teams and players.

I entered into the job market, in my senior year, working after school and on weekends in a stock room at a large department store. Of course back then, in the early seventy's, for a high school student to have fifty or one hundred dollars in their pocket was a rarity. I would, of course, buy clothes but mostly gospel albums and Christian books. I always gave Mom part of my paycheck and most times she would hold on to it knowing I would come back and ask for it.

After graduating out of high school I began working at a plastics factory. There was dust everywhere we made the raw plastics from a powder form then it turned into granules and we also added hundreds of colors before we stored it in our warehouse to be shipped out.

I became good at more than seven different factory positions and my income doubled in a few short years. Again, the Favor of God and His Anointing was on my life and that inspired me to stay focused and succeed in areas of my life although, there was still crumbs of guilt, shame, and condemnation that I had to eliminate out of my life.

Even with all of that going for me, there were many times that I thought that I was a failure by allowing the enemy to show me all of my bad traits and not any of my good traits. Not realizing that God only sees the good in us so I had to learn to see myself as He sees me. That is what would rid me of the guilt, shame, and condemnation.

I was making real good money for just coming out of high school and still living at home in my parents house. My Dad seen to it that the boys would give Mom a set amount of money every time we had a pay day. I always enjoyed doing for my Mom and still do I'm glad my Dad made giving money to her mandatory because this developed a sense of responsibility.

A few months later I bought my first car and the upkeep of an automobile took time a lot of money. Not so bad though because Daddy made us responsible to fix our own cars. Fixing my own car was fun and dirty but also rewarding to know that I knew how to solve mechanical problems. Now Daddy wouldn't do the work but he would coach me through making sure I was doing the right thing by using the right tools and buying the right parts.

By the time I had purchased my third vehicle I could rebuild a motor. I remember replacing water pumps, master cylinders, radiators and all the hoses, valve cover gaskets, even replacing universal joints on my drive shaft although, changing the oil and doing tune-ups were easy common practices. I also remember disassembling a carburetor cleaning it in gasoline; replacing springs, levers, and filters then assemble it back together.

Whenever I would come across something difficult guess who I'd call? You're right, Daddy! Again, he made me do the work and I didn't mind as long as it was done right. However, the amount of money saved from doing my own work was of course in the thousands on a yearly basis.

I remember the long talks Daddy and I would have during the many hours we spent working on cars. It seems like I got more out of helping him work on his car than working on mine. Daddy loved giving advice and what father doesn't love giving advice to his children. No matter what mood he was in we could always get good conversation out of Daddy, he loved to talk. Especially if he was upset with you this was a good way to back on his good side just help him do something rather he needed the help or not. And if you kept doing something wrong he would tell you "step aside" then he'll do it, I hated those words. But this was another good reason to watch and learn.

At the Plastic Factory my shift started at four o'clock pm and lasted until twelve midnight. I liked working that shift oppose to working the morning shift simply because it was a lot easier to locate enough forklifts with less people walking around. So it would be quicker for us to store materials away in the warehouses.

Of course by midnight on a Friday this ended our work week and it did not bother at all to know I had off until Monday at four o'clock pm. What I thought was also good when working the third shift which was twelve midnight to eight a.m. We would get off Friday morning and not having to be back until Sunday at midnight, almost like having three days off.

Another advantage for working the afternoon shift was I enjoyed going for long drives and this time of night there was very little traffic and you could slow down and time the traffic lights and get green lights most of the time. With gospel music playing in my eight track tape player me singing praises to God sometimes riding and singing until two or three o'clock in the morning. Driving my nineteen sixty seven Pontiac Catalina four barrel carburetor three hundred fifty horse power engine, for those who understand engine sizes. I always kept that light brown tan interior clean and, of course, in good running condition.

Sometimes I would take drives during the week, but mostly on the weekend, and go on the out skirts of town and enjoy the snow covered trees that covered the roads and the snow on the roads seems like driving on white carpet. I guess this must've been where I developed a love for driving.

My Mom was over the Usher Team in the church and she needed more male ushers on her Team and asked if I would help, I jump at the idea. Mom also thought it would be an inspiration for the other young people to get involved in church activities. Short time after that, other young men became involved in the choir, ushering, and teaching Sunday school.

Mom has a style and a smooth grace where she could get people to do things rather they wanted to or not. She cared a lot for everyone who was on her Team as though they were family members and actually they were. I admire so much the passion Mom has for people she has the most electrifying and tender smile that sends a loud message of love not to mention that her smile always said that she cares. She also knew how to put her foot down if it was necessary, raising five boys she couldn't be a pushover.

By staying busy in church ushering and singing in the choir we often traveled to other cities to sing regularly. Not only were there church services at our church but locally I attended other churches on a regular basis. I loved so much going to the different church conventions out of town and singing in their choirs.

We would only rehearse for a few hours everyone coming together from all over the state maybe sixty to seventy voices coming together for the final service of the night. Singers my parents age or older who sung in the choir were a strong inspirations to me.

Choir members can be symbolic to a team of athletes everyone has a part to play by singing in the right note so collectively we would sound like one voice. What an experience for me I learned so much about the different song arrangements the meaning behind the words that I was singing what a blessing and an experience for me I would do that all over again immediately.

I finally moved out from my parent's house into my own apartment for a short time, then got married and we rented a two bedroom house for about two years, after that we bought a home.

It was a small new sub-division with about fifty houses. Behind the house past the back yard there were acres of land that was used for growing corn. During the winter months or on the off season of growing corn people would ride their dirt bikes and snowmobiles on these open fields.

The house was a two story split level home when you entered through the double front doors onto the ceramic tile landing. There were four steps leading up into the living room, dining room, and kitchen. As you reach the top of the stairs and off to the left is approximately a thirty feet hallway branched off are two bedrooms and a full bathroom. There were four more steps coming off the landing leading into the basement after walking through the door and off to the right was the family room, straight ahead was a half bath with a shower. Off to the left of the door way was the laundry room and in front of the laundry room was the master bedroom with a walk in closet.

About a year after being in the new house my wife had our first child a handsome and strong baby boy, he is now thirty-six years young.

I enjoyed having family members and church members over for dinner mostly during the holidays. Seeing them enjoying themselves gave me such a pleasure to know I could offer what I had to make people comfortable.

Things were going pretty good I had bought a brand new nineteen seventy-six Chevy Nova off of the showroom floor. It was a hatch back with folding back seats (that added more to trunk space) cream color body with a light brown vinyl roof and tan color leather seats.

After approximately three years of having all this and at the age of twenty five in February of nineteen seventy eight, I left all this behind and enlisted into the United States Navy.

I was stationed Great Lakes, Ill., located right outside Chicago, I was in Great Lakes for Boot Camp and it was right on the water with the strong cold breezes in February. The most challenging part about Boot Camp was shoveling layers of snow off the sidewalks before breakfast. At least at home Mom would see to it that we got something hot into our stomachs before shoveling the snow off the long driveway.

Boot Camp lasted for three months which was in April and it had warmed up a lot. I went back home for a month and during this time I had orders to work out of the Recruiting Office downtown. All I did was sit around the office and maybe answered the phones and listening to the older and experienced Sailors told their sea stories. One thing I found out in Boot Camp from our Company Commander that Sailors don't mind stretching the truth and they are great story tellers especially when they have an audience.

The personnel at the Recruiting Office really didn't want me to get involve with their day to day operation. They just wanted me to relax and take it easy maybe answer the phones or tell a potentially new recruit of my Boot Camp experience which mostly consisted of academics. There were stiff penalties for falling asleep in class and why not we were being taught things that could save a life. Simply put, I need to know I could depend on my shipmate in a time of crisis and they could also depend on me.

I still remained excited about going to my first ship, called the U.S.S. Garcia a small battleship better known as a frigate with about one hundred fifty guys which I had orders to be stationed on located at the Shipyard in Brooklyn, New York.

But first I had to go to the Navy Base in Norfolk Va. for what the Navy called "A" school to learn the Navy system of their Supply Department. School lasted for about six weeks and I graduated with a ninety-eight percent grade average in a class of about thirty other Sailors. It seemed to go fast once everyone got settled in and took their studies seriously, after just getting out of Boot Camp which was mostly academics. Little did we know that these classes were the platform or the starting point for our actual duties that we were to perform on the ship.

It was easy to get distracted from our studies being that Norfolk Va. Naval Base is one of the largest if not the largest Naval Bases in the United States. It seemed the Naval Base covered an extreme large portion of the city. Seeing new faces was not unusual for the locals and it impressed me for the respect we got from them. It was like I was wearing a sign saying, "I'm new to this, please help me" and even on the Base the personnel was most accommodating when assisting us in our affairs. Just when I became comfortable with the area and acquainted with the city it was time for me to go.

After about a month of taking it easy at my hometown and finishing school in Norfolk Va. I finally arrived at the shipyard in Brooklyn, New York. The ship was small or better known as a Naval Frigate everything was so compacted but neatly organized.

The sleeping quarters was the size of a normal bedroom sleeping about ten to twelve guys. The beds were in columns of threes attached to metal post and the post was mounted into the floor, a lot different from my master bedroom. We had a stand up locker and the top part of our bed opened up into another locker, again, way different from my walk in closet. One small office space about half the size of a normal bathroom would represent a whole department. I also noticed that every bit of space was utilized for something.

For the next four years I'd have to live by minimizing my space to only arms length. So I'm thinking, "What in the world did I get myself into?" Another important fact, the food was excellent the Navy have some of the best cooks in the world. We received breakfast, lunch, and dinner seven days a week every week of the year. There were additional meals during the late hours of the night if we had to work. Our meals, our mail, and our pay are something you could depend on no matter what was going on.

It wasn't long before I became adjusted to Navy life the customs of respect for our superiors and personnel in authority was highly enforced. I understood this matter of respect that my superiors and people in authority were to receive and chalked it up for another level of discipline or maturity. But if the truth be told; How could you receive respect if you didn't give respect? I can't receive anything different from what I'm giving good or bad.

I quickly learned the urgency for safety and how important it was to do something right the first time, doing something the wrong way could result in someone getting hurt, seriously injured, or even killed. No one wants to be guilty of such a tragedy, so to avoid that our first thought was "safety first," again another level of discipline or maturity.

It was normal to get up at four or five in the morning to get cleaned up before breakfast then we had roll call. At roll call we were given instructions for our daily operations and information of the upcoming events, deployment dates, and destinations of these deployments and then we would start our work day.

After our wok day had ended, of course, we would go out in the town and why not. This is New York City some of the world's best entertainment and sporting events comes through New York. I was fortunate to see a professional basketball game at Madison Square Garden between the New York Knicks and the Philadelphia 76er's. What a thrill to be in the same room with these legendary Hall of Fame Athletes.

When on 42nd street I couldn't help but look around at all of the tall and fine buildings, just like a tourist. The sidewalks, the subways, the traffic in the streets were just as crowded at one o'clock in the morning as it is at three o'clock in the afternoon. So many people everywhere there was no getting away from them. I can't remember ever seeing the same person twice it seemed everyone was a stranger there was no end to new faces. A person could get somewhere faster on the subway than they could in a car or even in a cab and not be concerned about parking.

It wasn't long before I became involved with a beautiful young lady from Brooklyn she used to work in the shipyard. And I use to see her going to and leaving work. Even in men's work clothes that she would wear her small frame would still show and I see her distinct beauty and it captivated me.

We would catch the Ferry to Coney Island, we would go to Time Square, and even Central Park was still safe back then. We would go to the gym located in the shipyard and part of the Navy facilities where she taught me how to play hand ball a common New York activity. This was the first time I ever played and I can't remember ever playing again. I don't remember who won the most games, we were just having fun although, I do remember not being able to play at our full potential because we were laughing so much.

Finding a place to eat was never a problem it was just deciding where to eat and how much to spend. I quickly fell in love with New York's glamour it's variety of entertainment, its atmosphere of excitement, and being with the finest lady in Brooklyn, all of that spelled fun for me. I enjoyed myself so much I felt like a child at a three ring circus just enjoying one event after another, never a dull moment and never running out of things to do.

After six months in Brooklyn I regretfully had to say "good bye" to this beautiful sweet young lady, to her Mom, and to her sister. As much as I tried I could never get back to Brooklyn to see her. I still remember that sad moment and often wonder how she is doing, even though, the relationship was short she made a big impact in my life.

For years I could still see her electrifying golden smile; to hear her laughter added music to the moments we shared; and see the innocence of love and the sincerity in her eyes. How could I not love a lady with such beauty and for me to carry the fragrance of her charm for all these years? I just pray that you are doing well and you are fulfilling the destiny that God has placed in your life. Amen!

We were off to sea for Guantanamo Bay, Cuba for thirty days of testing the ships functions and for combat training it took about a week to get there.

Our daily routine was, at four a.m. every morning we were untying the ship and pulling away from the pier to go to sea and start our training and most times returning after dark. This was supposed to be a thirty day operation but it turned into three months because the instructors wanted everything done perfectly, and why not? We're defending the greatest country in the world and we needed to be perfectly trained to perform the task. It was a matter of pride, honor, and integrity and this is what gave each department the initiative to pass all the tests.

However a sense of accomplishment made us proud to have passed the many tests and now being ready for battle we were trained to respond quickly and efficiently. When certain alarms would be sounded we had but a few minutes and maybe seconds to get to our designated stations. Even though it seem like a race but being orderly and safely moving about avoided chaos and tragedies.

Plus the fact that most of Cuba, at that time, had many restricted areas and we wanted to get back to the States and be in unrestricted areas. You really don't know how sitting down in a restaurant and having a good meal is missed, or go shopping to the store of your choice until you have been placed in a situation as this. After being permitted to leave Guantanamo Bay, Cuba we headed for the Naval Base in Charleston, South Carolina this was to be our home port.

After about a year had passed, and I had been experiencing the busy city in Norfolk Va. and also living the busy and exciting life in Brooklyn then months of seclusion in Cuba for training, and getting use to Charleston took some time. And I think after returning a few times, when we had finished our deployment is when I began to reluctantly get adjusted to another military town. Of course, I had no idea this town would become my home after my military life would end, although, my plans were to go back to Ohio.

Our ship received orders for a six month deployment in the Mediterranean Sea mostly going through more maneuvers, more training and in formation with other ships. It was then when I learned why ship formation was needed and how important it is.

I remember coming up close to an Aircraft Carrier this massive metal structure seem to be one hundred times the size of our little Naval Frigate ship. It was like a bicycle coming along side a forty passenger bus. Aircraft Carriers sometimes have a population of about four to five thousand Sailors that was more than the population of my high school. Their flight deck might relate to the size of three football fields and this is just the landing strip for the airplanes. It's built into about eight, nine or more stories high and the same size or bigger than a high school. To think God gave man the knowledge and ingenuity to construct such a massive water vessel moving in the water at twenty to thirty miles per hour is amazing. Just imagine a high school or a mall going down the street at twenty or thirty miles per hour.

About another a year had passed and I began to feel comfortable fitting into the Navy way of life and being recognized as a team member. Many times those of us who had some experience we began to mentor or coach the new combers. I could sympathize with a young eighteen year old being away from home for the first time. One thing for sure is that if we could give this guy the right information concerning Navy life. The more comfortable they became and the easier it was for them to do their job.

Through the course of my four year enlistment I remember going to places like Spain, Greece, Puerto Rico, Bermuda, Italy, France, Australia, and Africa just to name a few places and seeing the different cultures was intriguing for me. I finally got a chance to see the Leaning Tower of Pisa and the massive golf courses in Bermuda. I seen the Rock of Gibraltar we also went through the Suez Canal with temperatures were in the nineties without any breeze in January. These are just a few of the major spots that come to mind, of course, there's more and I'm not eliminating them intentionally.

There is no way a price tag that could be put on what I was being exposed to in the way of how strong and organized the Navy system is. And all the different places I had been overseas and in the United States. That's why some thirty plus years later it is easy to remember some of the details and the major highlights, it's almost like re-living these experiences.

All of what I'm writing is actually the truth there's nothing in this book that's untrue, nothing is being made up. Sharing with the world in love is my only objective with this book and somehow people will see my mistakes and by the help of God learn from them.

Almost two years had passed and I was serious needing a relationship with God. So I thought I would study the Nation of Islam and was impressed how they displayed boldness. And they take order and discipline to a whole new level more than what I had known. However, I knew in my spirit this was not the direction God wanted me to go. But still the idea of having another relationship with God would lay dormant, and I, once again was in search for something to fill that void.

I allowed depression to set in, I didn't want to socialize any more, I would volunteer to work the night shift just to be alone, and I didn't feel worthy to be close to God, so I figured why not take to the streets again.

First it started with me going to the night clubs in these varies countries. Of course who goes to a club and not drink, then, here come the pretty women, and somehow cigarettes came back into existence. I didn't have to go this route but it seemed to be the quickest and easiest way out, or so I thought, so I indulged into whatever it took to submerge my feelings. Did I feel comfortable living this kind of life? No! At this point guilt, shame, and condemnation had begun to control my emotions and I tried to hide it with my wrong doings.

I came up with this idea that I would go out by myself and not hang out with the guys, simply because if I didn't want to drink myself silly I didn't have to give answers why. Of course, the rule was if someone came back after being on the town and that person was not talking loud, could barely walk, or didn't vomit on themselves they didn't have a good time. If I just wanted to sit in front of a water fountain for hours and think then I would. If I wanted just to go window shopping for hours, while again thinking, then I would.

We would get strict orders not to go into the bad areas which would be considered high crime or drug areas. Sailors would go into these areas and get beat up, robbed, or sometimes arrested for their wrong activities I never heard of anyone being killed.

By me going out by myself didn't change my activities I just partied with different people that were of the same mindset. Despite the strict orders to stay away from certain dangerous areas I still went straight to those areas where we were told not to go by myself. I would not recommend this type of disobedience for anyone else it may not turn out the same way. However, I had fun meeting people and having a good time and not even understanding the language. I was invited into people houses, went to the clubs with them, and going to restaurants just taking all kind of chances.

I guess what helped me the most, besides God being secretly with me, I wasn't afraid I was just as friendly with these people like I had known them my whole life. And after a while this became a way of life for me whenever I went to a strange country of city.

You have to understand that I grew up not experiencing crime or violence. I always heard it from other people's perspective, somehow God always saw fit for violence not to be part of our family's life. So I didn't see crime when I went into these areas; I didn't see bad; I didn't try to get over on these people. They bought things for me and I bought things for them. And this is not just in a few areas but in every area I went into.

Looking back at the various situations I placed myself into I know God was with me. Somehow I felt safer in the streets overseas half way around the world than I did state side. Hmm? Figure that! If the truth just be told, the same Hand of God's Protection that was keeping me safe half around the world is the same Hand of God's Protection that keeps me safe in my living room.

During my four years in the military there were a lot of good things I learned one of them was to be organized with my affairs, how to finish things that I started and do it correctly. By me working in the Supply Department I learned and became good at bookkeeping, inventory, and purchasing which nowadays it comes under the umbrella of Logistics. Our Department received the Supply "E" award which simply means we were efficient in our work and met or exceeded all standards of Navy Regulations. Not to mention "bragging rights" and "why not" we earned it.

We often work seven days a week rather as sea or pier side depending on what the work load called for. Promotions or advancements in rank were granted from passing a series of test with detailed questions about your job knowledge. We also became trained in fire safety; in weaponry; also how to receive fuel and transport supplies at sea. Receiving fuel and transporting supplies at sea was the most challenging it involved precision timing and maximum safety practices. On smaller ships everyone on board became involved in this operation the more people involved the less time it took and safer the operation. On larger ships usually it was enough personnel in one or two departments to safely and quickly handle the operation. Sometimes questions about fire safety, weaponry, and replenishing supplies were on the test also.

During my four years of Naval duties I made it to the rank of E-4 which was like a promotion in rank every year, advancements would have continued if I had decided to reenlist but I decided on an honorable discharge and start another part of my life. Now after looking back finishing sixteen more years of military might not have a bad idea. Keep reading and you'll see what I mean!

CHAPTER 4

GOD GIVES US HIS RESTORATION

After being discharged from the military, of course, I didn't go back to my hometown in Ohio. Plus, after seeing the many different parts of the world and warmer climates I decided to stay in Charleston, SC.

Until I was able to find work I lived off of the money I had accumulated from the Navy which wasn't much. I was accepted as a youth counselor at a Youth Center working the midnight shift making only enough to pay rent and utilities.

Available job opportunities for veterans were not advanced like it is today or at least I was not aware of any programs that would get me an edge into the job market. Knowing what I know now, by me being fresh out of the military I qualified for Firemen, Law Enforcement, or the world of Logistics.

But just like if my Dad would have played professional sports or if I would have went into one of these professions. I could have missed out on something that would not eventually get me to this point. And Family let's face it, we all have looked back over our lives and wish we would have made different or better decisions. However, we learn how to deal with those decisions and move on to better grounds and brighter days.

After months of being in a money crunch, and again right out of the military, I got into the taxi business. I found out how I could make money everyday plus work my own hours. Quick money settled the money crunch plus from being in the military I became accustomed to working seven days a week and adjusting my own work hours was also a plus.

Soon five years of driving taxi became ten years and then fifteen years almost twenty years had come and went before realizing how far I was away from the job market with out any actual work experience. I had nothing to show for all the money that I made poor planning and a lack to prioritize got me into this situation, what a blow to my ego.

Another chance for inferiority to set in I almost believed I couldn't do anything else until I forced myself out of the business because of my drug habit. Approximately the last three or four years of being a cab driver I experienced a daily use for crack cocaine.

Now can you see why staying in the Navy would have been a better idea than going through this mess that I was involved in?

Can you imagine making eight hundred to a thousand dollars a week homeless living out of a car? After leaving the taxi business, I recall living out of a truck and even in a storage unit. Ignorance was my major way of thinking. How low must I go or how stupid must I become? Before coming to my senses and decide to remove myself from this living hell.

I finally got to the point where I was loosing at everything I would put my hands on. I couldn't hold a job for no longer than thirty days. The things that I said that I would never do for survival I did. I was totally at my end and if I would have gone any longer, living the way I was living, death or prison was my only option, both to me seem similar.

Death, of course, is the absence of life and prison is the absence of social freedom. Numerous times God tried to get my attention but this one time God spoke to me and ask "what do you want to do" quickly I spoke out loud saying, "to live for Your Glory and Purpose." I honestly believe if I had not given God that heart felt answer this bad situation would have gotten worse.

A few days after Thanksgiving 2005 I walked approximately ten miles to a Drug Treatment Center, I was hungry, dirty, needing rest and medical attention because of the abuse I had put my body through. At one point in my diagnoses I had a fever of one hundred thirteen degrees and my heart rate was up to one hundred forty-three. And it took days for my vitals to become normal but being that the Center gave me plenty of liquids, decent food, and after resting I started to come around. Only by the Grace of God I didn't have a stroke or die of a heart attack. I stayed in the Drug Treatment Program for over three years.

Of course most of us have heard that we hurt the ones we are close to especially when our way of living leads to selfishness and that within itself is self destruction! Because sin makes people highly selfish it has us believing in that syndrome where "it's all about me" and no one else.

At the time of me doing my dirt (in my addiction) I was not aware I was deeply hurting my children, my parents, my siblings, cousins, aunts, and uncles the list just goes on and on. I think my Daughter was hurt the most because a large portion of Her younger years I was not in Her life. Maybe She will read this part of the book and it will bless Her. She's my only Daughter and I know She dearly loves me as I dearly love You, there's not a day that goes by when I don't think of You. I know I was wrong and I take full responsibility for my selfish actions. God has forgiven me; I have forgiven myself; I pray that You will forgive me as well. Again, I Love You! May God continue to keep You safe in His Peace so that You may walk in His Blessings Daily. Amen!

To my only Son, I'm so proud of Your musical gift and how God has developed You into a strong and fine Man of God. There were numerous times over the years I could have reached out for you and attempted to be a father but failed to do so, and for that I apologize. I also hope You will be blessed when You read this part of the book. I Love You! May You also Walk in God's Blessings Daily! I constantly pray for the both of You and that someday the three of us will meet again. Amen!

There were also people who I had developed strong relationships from church, people I grew up with, former classmates, co-workers, neighbors, and just everyday people I came in contact with. The count can range into the hundreds or even the thousands because I was well-known. Of course the people I tried to make amends to first were family members and even now some of them are not receptive. And for now that's alright because I caused that separation so it may take longer for some than others. As I continue to allow The Word of God to change me and for me to find more ways to demonstrate "Love."

I like the scriptures in Joel 2:25-26, And I will restore to you the years that the locust hath eaten, the cankerworm, and the caterpillar, and the palmerworm, my great army which I sent among you.

And ye shall eat in plenty, and be satisfied, and praise the name of the Lord your God, that hath dealt wondrously with you: and my people shall never be ashamed.

No way am I'm not justifying myself for my wrong doing, however this scripture shows us when we decide to put our life in God's Hands. His Mercy and Grace will work for us all we have to do is receive this Strong Promise.

I am the oldest of six siblings, five boys and one girl. My brother who is three years younger than I and who is the closes to me in age, he was emotionally and spiritually inspirational to me in a huge way in my early stages of my recovery while I was in The Drug Abuse Program. At the time he was the only Family Member who knew what I was going through.

Although he did not know the pain of my recovery however he understood my severe mood swings. He, also, would bring me up to date of how everyone was doing and filled me in on the years that I had missed with the family, friends, and classmates. We would talk for hours almost daily; he always found time to speak with me even though he worked fulltime as a truck driver and supported his family of four.

Upon going through the process of my recovery/deliverance, I instantly began to set boundaries around myself and enjoyed doing so. I knew I couldn't go anywhere near those areas and be associated with those people that kept me in my addiction, which carried extreme bondage. The enemy tried to get me to reason with my flesh thinking, "awe just go ahead and do it one more time no one will know." But I used The Word against those thoughts and I cut it loose because I wanted out and wanted to stay out.

Now after six years of being free from the addiction the enemy still tries to tempt me to go in areas of destruction. I've learned to take those temptations and use them for "stepping stones." A lot of odds were against me but I was determined to live and not die. Even people that was in authority and knew my situation would speak negative words as to try and get me to falter.

Countless times the Holy Spirit would inspire and directed me to do positive things which mostly involved helping people. One of my favorite pass times would be writing on the computer at the library which is where I started writing this book. Then I would get involve with different activities mostly around the church, which is a good place to stay busy. The Holy Spirit knew I had to stay busy but busy doing the right thing. I stayed busy when I was on the other side of the fence sometimes going days without sleep or food.

Also, I started being around people who were going places; influential people you were led by the Holy Spirit and the Fruit of The Holy Spirit evident in their life. It was a lot of work and I'm still working The Word in every area of my life with maximum results, God's results.

You would have to understand my triumphs came in small increments and what some people would call daily routines these routines were my goal setters. Such things as; being able to eat more than one meal everyday; able to keep my hygiene up with one or more showers daily; what a simple thrill to wear clean clothes everyday. I could open a bank account and keep money in it without being overdrawn. I could pay my cell phone bill for a year without it being shut off. I could pay rent without any worries of getting an eviction notice. And keep the electricity on without any interruption in service. Even go to the supermarket and spend one hundred to two hundred dollars on food and still have money left over. These are some of the small things I was able to accomplish once I turn my back on the dark side of living and start to apply God's Word in all areas of my life.

Also understand my parents gave us (six children) the best of everything we did not go lacking for anything. We had new clothes, expensive furniture, beautiful house, nice cars etc. I had a good taste of what fine living was all about, and for me to have to resort to the "scrum of the earth" for survival was totally insane. My parents would have never dreamed that one of their children would live such a life of filth.

It took ten years or better for me to decide to make a change. Most of that time, I tried to camouflage my challenges until one day I had to take the mast off. At that point pride, embarrassment, and prestige were out the window I wanted help and needed it "yesterday or yester-year." Let me say it like this, "I was tore up from the floor up" and needed a "check up from the neck up."

There was nothing good about my situation although by taking one thing at a time and changing that one thing became more successful for me. Even when we look at the list of corrections we need to make with ourselves just by making one corrections at a time is a lot easier than grabbing a handful and possibly not making any corrections. That is where small increments of progress become evident this principle can be applied in many areas of living; businesses, academics, relationships, work ethics, church duties, etc.

So as I allowed, The Word of God to transform my thinking; and with me being persistent in The Word of God my thought life began changing my desires then my decisions changed which gave me new directions.

Through reading and meditating on Gods Word I had easily started moving towards the path that He designed specifically for me to go. One of the things that I would do is read a chapter a day from the Book of Proverbs according with the day of the month. I would repeat the process over and over each month in just a few short months purpose was once again birthed in me.

I could set Godly goals and achieve them such as; I could pay my tithes and offering and have plenty left over; I could reunite with family members and we would rejoice in each others accomplishments. I could laugh again and my smiles became genuine and not fake. I could walk around with my chest out and my head held high. I could look people in their eyes when talking to them, and not hold my head down because of embarrassment. Love once again was rekindled in me for people and for the things I became involved in. Staying planted in God's Word gave me my dignity and self respect back I could love myself again which allowed me to love others.

I learned from reading the Book of Proverbs those chapters cover finances, relationships, work ethics, but mostly Proverbs began to shape my character and I began to get my sense of self-worth back again. I became so excited with this new found man or this man that was always there but lying dormant, I didn't know God and I could have so much fun. He talking to me and me talking to Him I didn't know God could become my "Best Friend" my confidence level was and still at an "All Time High."

I also learned how to develop strong Godly Character by reading and study the books of Matthew, Mark, Luke, and John. This part of the Bible shows how Jesus carried out His Ministry and the many lives He affected. We see the attitude of Jesus in adverse situations, how He kept a positive attitude and constantly kept the devil under His feet through applying Gods Word. We see the many times Jesus would take challenges and with simplicity of The Word and The Anointing on His life made deliverance after deliverance just like what He wants us to do with the life we now live.

I knew then and I know now that I am the "Righteousness of God" because He has taken all unrighteousness from me. I John 1:9 "… He is faithful and just to forgive our sins, and to cleanse us from all unrighteousness." I no longer had to be led astray because of guilt, shame, and condemnation.

When I started fasting and praying, seem like things would speed up and I would get raises on the job with promotions and favor in so many areas of my life. Things were happening at such a rapid pace, God's Favor became a daily habit for me to experience.

So, if we "present our bodies a living sacrifice, holy, acceptable unto God, which is our reasonable service." Romans 12:1 Why not stay around because, "God will open you the windows of Heaven, and pour you out a Blessing, that there shall not be room enough to receive it." Malachi 3:10 Sounds like a good plan to me! Our employer can't do that, the government can't do that, Mom and Dad can't do that. So, why not do The Word with love and devotion unto God and it's a guarantee God's going to do His part and reward us with His Promises.

I'm so excited to reach out and encourage someone to go through God's process of renewing our mind in The Word. You may not have been involved in a difficult situation such as I have. However, the process of mind renewal is the same method or principle. You may have an eating disorder; credit card debt; marriage problems; or maybe just needing additional direction from God. His Word covers and delivers us from any and all obstacles, but it all starts with our way of thinking. Like me, I was to the point where I didn't want to listen to anyone; hard-headed, stubborn, and determined to do it my way.

At the time I wasn't aware what possessions I was entitled to or what power I could attain by doing The Word. But, a decision had to be made on my part for any change to take place, rather good or bad.

We may think that we can help a person who may be having serious challenges with their life. But, until that person is ready to turn away from their dilemmas and go into the right direction we have to totally operate in The Wisdom of God in dealing with this kind of an individual. As not to be an enabler to them and assist or cater to their dilemma, I didn't need sympathy and excuses to stay the same way. I needed "tough love" in taking responsibility for my actions and to prove myself that I needed and went after a change for the better things. I was the only person that could help me and once I helped myself than people came to my aid because of my sincerity.

CHAPTER 5

GOD GIVES US LEVELS TO ATTAIN

When I was in the Drug Treatment Program I would find ways or opportunities to spend time with The Father. Because my sincerity levels was way beyond anyone in the complex because I realize who I am in Christ and where I was going. It seemed the more I would get away and spend time with God the easier the day would go.

When I would be at work and was glad when lunchtime came so I could get away by myself, just to read a few scriptures. Or just, Thank God for the way my day was going. After I had finished a days work, I would rush back to the facility get cleaned up go to my room and dive back into The Word for hours. Often times missing meals, no phone calls, and no visits just me and God.

If I was out running errands and in a line waiting for something I would begin praying and quoting scriptures and, of course, praying that the line would go quicker. As I was going down the street en route for somewhere, is another way I would sneak some time to spend with Him. As I was going through my daily duties at work, there were periods when I would be by myself, I would think on Him and sometimes I couldn't hold back the tears.

"This book of the law shall not depart out of thy mouth; but thou shalt meditate therein day and night, that thou mayest observe to do according to all that is written therein: for then thou shalt make thy way prosperous, and then thou shalt have good success." Joshua 1:8, this scripture was then and is still a big part of my life.

Many times we may think that spending a lot of time with God may not be normal. But when we were on the other side of the fence we thought it was normal to keep our refrigerators full with beer. Spend all day watching television, playing cards for hours, or listening to music that was not appropriate to build positive mindset. How many times did we say we were shopping too much or going to the night club too much?

All I know is that, I went all out while doing my dirt why not go all out for doing the right thing in God. I mean we get long life; help in time of trouble; nothing but blessings operating in our life; our marriages go through levels of being harmonious; I get unlimited favor these are just a few of the benefits. But on top of all that I get to show someone else how they can get "There" because together we can do more for God, God loves team work in His Kingdom. Look at the team work Jesus and His Disciples had.

I had started to notice a gradual change at our group home a different type of atmosphere had started to take over. Guys were starting to get jobs, we started to get along with each other a lot better, some guys started to go to church with me. I had started to get raises and promotions on the job. I could just see the "Hand of God" all through the complex of the four different houses. I began to have more favor with the staff members; they would hold my meals when I had to come in pass dinner time. I was allowed to break curfew because of church services.

I guess when you see the "Power of God" come alive in your own life and in the lives of the people around you. Excitement is very easy; I was referred to many times as "Preacher" I loved being called that.

It wasn't a mystery that something wonderful was taking place in my life. A whole new direction was developing; my desires became pure and Christ-like; my outlook on the same things that I always looked at before, I looked at them differently.

Even down to some of my favorite television programs, they started looking obsolete and I couldn't enjoy them anymore. I could quickly see the wrong or right in a thing before getting involved. Certain music became highly selective; I would only listen to Praise and Worship songs. I got the most from Praise and Worship songs during times of reading and praying. My spirit became very sensitive to situations; I could sense the realness in people very easy, almost too easy. I had started to think, is there anybody real anymore?

Then, I became sensitive in my selection of Men and Women of God that I would allow to preach to me or speak into my life. The Men and

Women of God I decided to accept as Spiritual Gifts, help me build my faith in ways I didn't think possible. I began to understand goal setting was unlimited; my dreams became more of a reality; I started to see myself prosperous again I just didn't want my accomplishments to end. What I was trying to do is flood my life in all areas with God's Word being at home, going back and forth to work, in my conversation, in my reading, and the things I watch on television had to be wholesome.

As time has gone by, over the years, Father God becomes more and more real to me. I have learned and accepted that The Father is everything to me and even more than I could imagine. I've seen "His Hand" on countless occasions; rearranging things in my favor, in keeping my body free from sickness and disease.

I began to heavily get into areas of searching for better health so I began to do research in the areas of nutrition and found what foods were best for my blood type and more studying on different herbs that I needed to rebuild my system. Of course, there were physical impurities that needed to be flushed from my body. If the truth be told, if I would have allowed these impurities stay in my body my illness could have resulted in death in the upcoming years.

Many different medications I was getting through the facility these medications were giving me harsh side effects and I noticed how the medications were affecting others. Extreme mood swings, increase or decrease in eating habits, even their ability to finish sentences would come and go. So I'm thinking; how is this any different from "street drugs?"

All I know is that I wanted no part of it, seemed to me that we were coming out of one bad situation into another bad situation. How could medication that was so controlling be good for our bodies? Most times they needed more medications because of the side effects of the first medication. It had got to the point where I seen some guys with ten to fifteen pill bottles. In most cases they were required to take these medications so they could receive medical services or be compensated financially. My case was different all I had to do was stay clean from drugs and alcohol, and random drug testing for everybody was frequent.

I began to look at how people in the Bible lived hundreds of years with little or no medical assistance, because there were doctors who practice medicine. I found out there's a powerful herb they used called "hyssop" this herb eliminates about every ailment that we may ever encounter. I was amazed at what this legal and powerful herb does it also can be used as a cleaning agent and I found all of this on the internet.

I also focused in on why our relatives were dying in their sixty's and seventy's years of age which according to Bible Living Standards this is a young age. We had eight relatives die in a five year span and as I looked closer at their lifestyle; poor eating habits and no exercise is what took them out at an early age.

I learned to avoid a lot of late night eating; eating and not being hungry; eating a lot of fried and greasy foods. When we eliminate fresh fruits and vegetables from our daily meals and without exercising all of this takes a toll on our bodies and gives us bad health. Eating cannot be our favorite past time however we must see eating only for nutritional purposes when hungry.

The more research I gathered the more changes I did in my own life concerning my health. For almost ten years now I've been avoiding bad eating habits and it wasn't easy because what I thought was alright was all wrong. And for the pass five or six years I've relied on herbs, minerals, and a better choice of natural foods.

One truth you may encounter when deciding to eat healthy and that is, healthy food cost more than unhealthy food. I like to say it like this, we are going to pay sooner or later and I would rather pay now and enjoy life. Than to pay for medications and suffer with the side effects and the price of doctor's bills. Also consider the hardship we bring on our families when our poor health carries us into physical or mental limitations and sometimes death.

I'm in my fifty's and soon will be in my sixty's I ride bicycle, play basketball, and a lot of walking. For years I would tell myself that I love water and now I even find myself drinking water through the night. I'm not on any medications and I don't have any body ailments or any physical limitations.

At one point I had challenges hearing out of my right ear and with just a few short months of taking "hyssop" my hearing is back to normal. I had notice I had to set my volumes lower when listening to music or watching television. At one point I had some skin irritations and by being consistent with the herbs these irritations has went away. I began to notice my sense of taste and smell became keener. My appetite and taste for unhealthy foods was no longer a part of my life.

It seems like the older I get the better I feel and the more I can do. And I can see why this would be true because the older we get the wiser and more informative we become. I set goals and push myself to achieve them for purposes of having better health. If it were possible I would love to play football again!!! Yeah I said it so laugh with me!

I began to listen to Doctors who believed in herbals who would most times teach on Christian Channels. This is when I first heard about eating the right foods for your blood type. They also mentioned drinking unlimited amounts of water increases natural skin color, and it keeps kidneys flushed out. Another key fact, is eating smaller portions is better for our digestive system; eating two to four small meals, through out the day, is better than eating one big meal. Our metabolism can better distribute the necessary nutrients into areas of our body when the food supply is minimal.

Experts say that it's perfectly normal to go to the bathroom after every meal. I like to think of it like this if we were to keep some kind of food in the refrigerator for weeks at a time. How gross this piece if food looks and smells in just a few short weeks. So, without being cleaned out regularly this same kind of food sits in our colon for years possibly turning into stages of cancer or maybe creating other health issues all because we failed to keep our digestive system clean by adhering to simple daily health tips (fiber).

These are the daily herbs and minerals that I take and the foods I eat: zinc, vitamin D, fish oil, hyssop tea and tablets, and hawthorn berries tablets. Again, the internet can inform everybody of the different ways these herbs and other herbs can reduce or eliminate health challenges.

I became accustomed to cooking with olive oil, drinking distilled water and green tea, using wheat flour and raw sugar, eating less fried foods, also eating brown wild rice and wheat bread. I have learned to eat more chicken, turkey, pork, and sea food. Beef and their by products didn't seem to agree with me. I also omitted late night eating and I only eat when I'm hungry and not because the food is there.

God will heal us when we exercise our faith and if the condition that God is healing us from is related to us not taking care of our bodies. He will still heal us simply because, "We Have The Kind of God Who *Gives*!" Then when we become healed, will we go back to the old habits of not taking care of our bodies? If we would listen to the Holy Spirit telling us how to protect our body's health then maybe we would not need a miracle of healing for ourselves but maybe a miracle of healing for someone else.

In III John :2 God says, "Beloved, I wish above all things that thou mayest prosper and be in health, even as thy soul prospereth. We see the first thing God mention was for us to prosper then health then our soul prospering. Do you think God knew that we needed good health so we can prosper? Yes! There is little or no prospering if our body is sick actually prosperity includes good health.

Now, I see it like this if I don't do the things to have and keep a healthy body then I won't do the things to have and keep a healthy soul, both intertwine with each other. How can I gain prosperity on my soul if my body is sick? So, it's safe to say that The Holy Spirit will lead us to areas of informing us for a healthier body just as He will lead us to scriptures for a better soul and mind renewal.

I speak and confess divine healing and health daily into my life and from this confession come avenues for me to take that will give me permanent health. This is where it all starts with our confession or the lack of our confession.

We have work to do for God and first the work starts with the person we see in the mirror. If we are not willing to do what is necessary for ourselves then; how can God trust us to do what is necessary for someone else? Our Ministry starts within the four walls of our home. Amen?

CHAPTER 6

THROUGH HIS WORD GOD GIVES US PRINCIPLES

We need to understand God has established Principles, Laws, and Standards through His Word. These statues are proven guidelines given to mankind to live by Kingdom Government. No obstacle can withstand His Kingdom and He has allowed us, as believers, to carry out "Precious Commandments" for our benefit and for our gain, which gives Him Glory. He gets the Glory when people see us operating in His Kingdom Government to have success. They might ask, "How did all this happen and where did all this come from?" With humility and a huge smile we reply, "My Father God Who is in Heaven made this all possible!" More importantly assure them that this success can happen for them.

God has a defined structure to His Plan of Kingdom Government which brings order, excellence, and increase. Without order there is chaos, confusion, and of course, deception. How can we expect to profit if we miss or eliminate the basic element "order."

The dictionary defines order as being, an established system; a prescribed form or customary procedure; a command given by a superior.

Of course, we know Father God is our Superior and His established system is for our advantage. He has prescribed procedures for us to have victories which are supposed to be the norm for us. Jesus proved this in His Walk with The Father in every aspect of His Life.

When Jesus fed the multitude in Matthew 14:19 the first thing He did, "He commanded the multitude to sit down on the grass." Order! Because the multitude obeyed the commandment of Jesus there was increase in food even more than they needed. Just think, if all those people came rushing at that food it would have been total chaos. Again, Jesus knew order was the best method for the multitude. I could almost hear the disciples telling the multitude, "If you all stay calm and do what He says you can get what we have, there's plenty for everyone." "Or, are they going to act stupid with disobedience starve and die or obey and live?" Hmm! Obey God and live! So, it's safe to say that levels of obedience get us our "breakthrough."

Allow me to elaborate a bit on "obey God and live." We see when Adam obeyed God in The Garden of Eden he and Eve lived well and not wanting anything. Of course, we know when they yielded to disobedience they withdrew themselves from God which led them to first a spiritual death and then the physical death.

The dictionary defines excellence as being; superior, first-rate, the state of quality of excelling or being exceptionally good.

Hospitality in the home should always bring a peaceful, comfortable, and a fun atmosphere. This is where productive or non-productive qualities originate in many or all cases we would have to think excellence in order to give excellence.

Knowing how to attain excellence takes training, experience, and exposure away from our environment on different or many levels. Paying close attention to varies types of upgrades and belief that these upgrades can and need to be part of our life. Being observant is a key element for us to be able to cultivate an eye for excellence no matter what area excellence needs to be used.

We may live in an apartment or in a trailer park but we keep dreaming of the five bedroom house and three car garage. And we leave dirty dishes in the sink, dirty shower all the time, and we don't keep our windows clean. Then someday the light comes on and we correct these areas which will lead us to attack other areas. Maybe we start paying our bills on time, also not being late when we have to be somewhere, we may upgrade our wardrobe. It's the little things like that which make a big difference in getting to our wealthy place.

However, order and excellence is not something you pull off the shelf when needed. It has to become a way of life. When we engage heavily in meeting these criteria's of order and excellence increase will not be denied. Excellence is just the mindset of a person who thinks and sees themselves as Royalty. Everything God does is of superior quality for thousands of years there's no day that is the same every minute of those days are also new that never before existed.

When God first made us He never intended us to die He designed us to live forever just like Him, in His image. But when sin came into the earth by way of Adam death showed up and tried to rob us of the life that God has given to us. God intended for us to be superior in our thinking and our doing. So, we can have the victories Jesus had, and even greater ones. God knew that we could not handle or carry the cares of this world. That's why He wrapped Himself up in Jesus to show us how effective His Word is in destroying the world of darkness.

The Bible says His Word is Truth. I'll take it a step further to say His Word is excellent and proven perfect. Psalms 18:30 says, "As for God, His Way is Perfect:" and in Psalms 19:7 states that, "The Law of The Lord is Perfect, converting (or restoring) the soul:" I just don't see how my life would be free from destruction if I didn't take His Word and apply His Word in areas where my thinking would line-up with His correction.

When I was growing up there were a lot of Godly Principles established in our household. My Dad was the "King of Order" and my Mom she is the "Queen of Excellence." Daddy made the rules, which gave "order" and Mom would see that it got carried out to the exact letter which gave "excellence."

With six of us, five boys and one girl there had to be a man like Daddy to keep things running smooth. At the time it didn't seem smooth, but Daddy was an Anointed Man of God. Daddy and Mom conditioned us for success Daddy kept Mom in the best of everything and neither did any of us go lacking for anything. He was a man who took care of his household and in all areas a perfect example of a Man of God, a Husband, and Father.

Even though, Daddy was firm with life's values; however, he was very flexible in his character. He understood some of his methods needed improving. Mom would suggest different ways of handling issues and together they came up with a solution that perfectly suited our family.

With a fourth grade education Daddy owned and operated a profitable Trucking Company. I noticed Daddy's diligence in his endeavor no matter how hard the obstacles became. He taught himself every phase of the business he didn't go to Trucking School which would have cost thousands of dollars. He acquired the book or books that were needed to teach him the many phases of the business, then he took the test and passed.

I assisted Daddy for a short time with his bookkeeping until he quickly caught on. Again, Daddy's flexibility in character paid off and we learned better methods and he became more profitable. The solid belief and diligence Daddy had about doing things brought order to another level. He had a full team of support behind him mainly God, Mom and his children. Mom and Daddy would look for ways to bless people. Even through all of that, he raised a family of eight people and paid off a house.

He left a legacy of passion, honesty, and trust. With me I developed a genuine passion for the things of God, Family, and People in general. I would find myself doing for others and never wanting to stop and looking for more ways to give to people. With the mindset as I'm doing it unto God.

Daddy never went back on his word when he believed he was right, neither was his words ever a lie. He was always happy never saying a negative word. He would get up in the morning singing, laughing, cracking jokes and just enjoying "Life." I cannot give God enough "Thanks and Gratitude" for giving me such a "Perfect Father."

The Bible says in Proverbs 22:6, "Train up a child in the way he should go: and when he is old, (mature) he will not depart from it" (meaning he will not leave the truth).

Even though, we may stray away there is a foundation of "truth" that has been established in us that will always bring us back to where we are suppose to be. That's not saying that a person should always be led away because some don't ever make it back, they die out there.

But as we live our lives the "correction of truth" always finds a way to straighten our direction. Or just give us a more defined method of how to get there. Sometimes God allows people to cross our path that will be instrumental in our direction.

The dictionary defines "maturity" as, to evolve toward or reach development; development of mental or physical growth. Both of these words evolve or development institutes a "process." However, in "mans thinking" it's believed we can peak out in our "maturity process." But, the "maturity" we gain from God's Wisdom and Knowledge is a "continuous process" God's Knowledge is endless and far exceeds human intellect. When we see the results we get from the anointing working through us we will gladly remain in the process.

Jesus said in John 7:38, "He that believeth on Me, as the scripture hath said, out of his belly shall flow rivers of living water." Rivers never dried up and they always get more water added to it from the rain, small streams or brooks. God is saying the same to us that we will always have enough to supply in any area of our lives or the lives of others. We turn on the process or we turn it off, of course, when we turn it off the river stops flowing but the river is always there waiting to be turned back on.

So, as we see again order, maturity, and excellence is being established through God's Truth. Be ever so watchful as not to get locked into the mentality that we have arrived to a plateau of completion.

CHAPTER 7

GOD GIVES US HIS KNOWLEDGE AND WISDOM

As we see in chapter one, we made a decision to come out of the kind of living that did not benefit us in any way.

We discovered after making the decision we began to apply the Word of God in all areas of our life. And The Word started to change our old way of thinking and The Word began to direct our thinking. New desires started to birth; our direction was now on a positive path; we became part of the solution instead part of the problem. We could see the "Hand of God" move in the lives of those around us.

With our new mindset we began to develop ourselves in The Word and The Word began to show us how to prioritize things in all areas of our lives one area "Order" and the other "Spirit of Excellence." We found out that the more "Order" was used the more "Excellence" was needed for us to become more complete and through daily practice this became a way of life and not just a one time occurrence.

While in The Drug Abuse Program, I had started to notice the things in my life that I thought were hard they turned out to be easy. I learned how to be a problem solver just by looking at a situation optimistically and quickly finding the solution. Little did I know that The Wisdom and The Knowledge of God was leading me to these various solutions. I found out going to the root of a thing would erase the problem completely. I would ask myself certain questions, "What made this happen? Or! What can I do to prevent it from happening again?" Most times just by staying calm in a tense situation always gives you a quick and easy out come. How you perceive a thing will determine the kind of result you'll get.

Please understand, Family, that challenges will come some may be in the form of temptation which is simply another test of our faith. Our response to the temptation will determine the outcome. I like to say this, "temptation tells me that I have something valuable and the tempter (devil) wants to steal it." It's not a bad thing to be tempted because Jesus was tempted but battled every temptation with The Word. James 1:12," Blessed (empowered to prosper) is the man that endureth temptation:" When temptation comes I like to use this scripture in Galatians 3:13, "Christ hath redeemed me (us) from the curse of the law," The curse of the law is sin and death so therefore this temptation (and I name it) is not a part of my life. Instantly this temptation leaves but I know it will return and I'll repeat it again. Not only how I perceive a thing determines the outcome but what words I speak gives me the results.

Knowing that temptations are just stepping stones to our next level which will also determine how faithful we have been with the Word of God in previous situations. So it's highly essential that we pass through every test so we won't have to take it again. I heard someone say that it's an "open book test" so failing is not an option.

Our levels of increase are determined by our levels of completion with our tests, we must also understand that increase from God comes in increments even though He "opens the windows of heaven." We direct how much or how little comes out for our increase. In Matthew 25:21 "thou hast been faithful over a few things, I will make thee ruler over many things."

God is looking for how loyal or faithful we have been over the things we already have before He allows more things to come into our possession. So, as we keep things in order and continue to follow in God's Truth we'll start to see or experience increase in bigger ways. The Holy Spirit will start to lead us in a certain direction to receive this increase. Some might say, "It's about being in the right place at the right time," I like to call it "having my steps ordered by God" Psalms 37:23.

I can't place enough emphasis on "position," my "position" in the right church; my "position" on my job; my "position" in my family; my "position" in society; and my "position" with people in general. All of which play an important part in limiting or not limiting what I receive.

We can't treat people like dirt and expect to receive anything from God. Our "Love" walk is the first thing that's going to be measured or tested. Having a genuine passion for people is a major way of life and

God wants us to cultivate it. Whatever God is going to give us part of it is for the benefit of people. So, if we are not passionate for people we will not obey His Voice when He asks us to bless them. If the truth just be told the more we bless people the more He blesses us.

God's Blessings

We see in John 10:10 "The thief (devil) cometh not, but for to steal, and to kill, and to destroy: I am come that they (the believer) might have life, and that they might have *it* more abundantly." The Amplified Bible says, "have it in abundance (to the full, till it overflows)." That scripture destroys the myth when people say God kills people.

We must know there are two kinds of death; death of a believer who is in God's Kingdom; and the death of an unbeliever who is outside of God's Kingdom. The believer surrenders their natural life for a physical death in order to live again after the physical death has occurred because we know that we are going back home in Heaven.

The unbeliever made some wrong choices in their life and some of their choices were connected to the curse. As mentioned before the curse is sin and death those choices are made against the blessing this is a choice to deny Jesus into our lives without Jesus in our lives sin runs rampant and the reward is death. Romans 6:23, "For the wages of sin is death; but the Gift of God Eternal Life through Jesus Christ our Lord." Why would a person not want to receive God's Gift of Eternal Life? So the fact remains that sin kills people, not God.

Also, in Deuteronomy 30:19 clearly states, "I call Heaven and earth to record this day against you, that I have set before you life and death; blessing and cursing; therefore choose life, that both thou and thy seed may live:" God will not choose for us however by us choosing life we operate the blessing and eliminate the curse.

Simply put, we have the reward of the choices we make rather life or death; blessing or curses not choosing a life in Christ is what robs us of the life that God wants us to have.

CHAPTER 8

GOD GIVES US PURPOSE OR ASSIGNMENTS

I started in the Hotel Industry through a Temporary Agency not knowing where I would fit in or how well I would adapt. Most of my adult life I acquired good work habits by being thorough and I learned to complete what I had started.

My first assignment, at the hotel, was taking trash to the dumpster and bringing dirty linen to the laundry to be washed. It was a lot of work and at a fast pace I needed to carry out my duties at a prescribed schedule. Among those duties I was responsible for keeping all the public areas clean, management quickly noticed my efficiency and diligence on my first day. The Hotel Management approached and asked if I wanted a permanent job, of course the answer was yes.

Shortly after that I had developed a routine that kept me on schedule and had extra time to assist other employees. So, once my ninety day contract had expired with the Temporary Agency I was put on the Hotel's payroll.

With some people going "above and beyond" in their work performance would be out of the question, but it came to be the norm for me. Management also noticed how I interacted with the Guest plus how helpful and courteous I was treating them. This sort of attitude was easy for me since I always could get along with people plus many times I would just put myself in their shoes and accommodate them according. I remember countless times Guest would call to the front desk in a rage about maintenance issue in their room when I got to their room and took care of the problem, by the time I was leaving their room the Guest and I would be laughing.

I would get tips just from giving the right information about a good restaurant or a place to shop. Or even pushing a button on a television or turning a switch on an air conditioner, I thought this was great. In just a few short months I was awarded Employee of the Month and then went on to receive Employee of the Quarter. Again, I thought this was great I was recognized for just doing my job plus having fun as I did it. Praise God! Was this another piece of "Heaven on Earth" or what?

Of course, certain privileges came with the recognition, our own parking space for a month; cash bonuses; we got to wear a pennant representing our achievements; our picture and name would be posted in the lobby by the front desk for Guest to see; and most times there were luncheons for this occasion because there were others who were recognized.

A position opened in the Maintenance Department and I was asked if I was interested, of course again the answer was yes. Again, I did not know how well I would adapt I knew it was less physical and more fundamental plus an increase in pay to do this kind of work.

Outside of changing a light bulb and unclogging a toilet I had no idea what I was walking into. All I knew is that I wanted to learn and it was a promotion for me from the Housekeeping Department.

I soon realize that extreme safety had to be practice on every level and in all areas of the Hotel so making repairs correctly was highly important. I also realized that people lives were in our hands depending upon how safe our Hotel was. It was also our job to prevent foreseen accidents and structural tragedies otherwise called preventive maintenance and this was done weekly. I had the kind of Supervisor who had patience with me and taught me all phases of the Maintenance Department.

I became good in electrical, plumbing, carpentry, and air conditioning in such a short time to the point where I got called upon more often than other workers. I had notice that I had developed a strong trait for being efficient. This is when I was awarded Employee of the Quarter and after about two to three months I could operate the night shift by myself. It was a good feeling to know I could be trusted and depended upon to take care of a Hotel with two hundred thirty-four rooms.

And even after going to the Maintenance Department I would still be called upon to help out in the Housekeeping Department. I just had the mentality as The Word states in Ecclesiastes 9:10, "Whatsoever thy hand findeth to do, do it with thy might." It did not bother me to come to work early and stay late or even come in on my day off and even now I'm still that way.

Often times I would go behind the scene of the Hotel and search out the condition of the fire extinguishers; forced myself to memorize all the electrical power sources and their shut-offs; became familiar with water shut-offs; learned the internet connections and how to reset the system, and what routers covered what areas. Along with learning the television cable system such as what problems we needed to handle or when to call the cable company. I took many visits to the boiler room to check the temperature and water pressure gauges; along with getting acquainted with the various water pumps and their functions. And learning how to read and operate the fire panel in case of a fire.

Thank God we never had any tragedies other than losing electrical power in bad weather until the generator came on and restored electricity throughout the Hotel.

I also learned what plumbing and electrical repairs on the grounds where of the City and not of the Hotel. About six months had passed when I didn't have to refer to my notes when it came to the familiarity of these major areas.

It may seem a lot to remember but when you are confronted with these areas five days a week, eight hours a day, month after month, and year after year it becomes second nature. Plus, our response to a crisis had to be quick, safe, and efficient just like when I was in the Navy.

I've had Supervisors to try and figure out what made me be so dedicated in so many areas. Of course, some people would see that dedication and would like to take advantage of you, although, I knew that and that didn't bother me. I just remained focused because I knew where I wanted to go and the techniques I needed to use to get there.

When they would try to give me the worse details and they thought I would make a mess of things. I would end up correcting, fixing, or repairing the problem, actually those difficult task help me to learn a lot quicker.

Many times I would be reminded of the story of Joseph in Genesis chapters 37-42. When his brothers beat him and left him for dead so that the animals would eat him; then they sold him to be a slave; if that wasn't bad enough he got framed for rape a crime he did not commit. While in prison he still was successful and became head of the prison.

As time went on Joseph became second in charge under Pharaoh in the land of Egypt. It was his job to distribute and sale the many goods and resources people needed to survive during the famine. It's a beautiful story of Joseph a strong-willed man of God stepping out of the box. And not settling for what man's injustice had done to him. But, by excelling in the path that God had provided for him and people benefited from his God given authority. Just like people benefitted from my sincere efforts because of the authority God had given me.

I've been in the Hotel business almost seven years and it's been such a blessing to me, I love this kind of work. I've learned so much about repairs and the wrong and the right way to do repairs, every day is different never having two days the same and the learning never stops. I've learned how to prioritize my work which helps me stay organized and this makes it more difficult to forget to do something.

I can see how these experiences have a big part to play in my development to walk in my purpose and fulfill my destiny. It gave me the mental discipline needed for not quitting even though I was confronted with quitting many times. I knew someday I would rank among the best of them in doing my craft. I had started answering question from different people about issues they had in their houses and from my advice it was corrected.

I went back to school and took a college course and acquired a certificate in heating air conditioning and ventilation. I've learned how to simplify even the hardest tasks, or so it seems hard. Sometimes when it seemed to be difficult, I would stay calm; step back; or even take a break to clear my head. Then allow The Holy Spirit to minister to me concerning this situation. Then go back to the job with the solution of how to repair a thing.

A lot of what I have gain through job knowledge came from The Holy Spirit. In Psalms 138:38 it says, "The Lord will perfect that which concerns me." This technique became a common thing with me until I became fearless and undefeated. There was nothing I couldn't do when it came to getting the job done.

Remember I was working the night shift alone and when I was in the Guest room needing to solve an issue immediately. Listening to The Holy Spirit was my best and only option, Thank God for His Holy Spirit

The point I'm trying to make is, when we become diligent about a thing and enjoy doing it. We'll have challenges however we won't be overcome by those challenges. Because of our passion for our work we'll be creative in our craft and find ways to improve our craft. I found myself going back in the maintenance logs from years ago and read what issues they were dealing with back then and how they solved them. To my surprising they were using the same method that The Holy Spirit had showed me. At this point all I could do is become full with gratitude for His leadership. Determination for accomplishments on a positive level was one of my major goals and stopping was not in my DNA.

By continually taking it to better levels will become part of our character and a way of life quitting or discouragement will not be entertained not for a moment. Because, we have centered all of our energy on being positive and taking things to the next level people might say, "How can you take those hard blows?" When we didn't even feel any blows or notice any adversity when we used that adversity as a stepping stone or as an inspiration to accomplish our task. Just like riding in our car and not noticing the wind passing by but staying focused on getting to our destination. The same scenario applies in whatever endeavor we desire to accomplish.

Now I can see how Joseph took his abuse, because he knew those uncomfortable situations were not a place where he was to stay. Often times through his process God assured him that He was by his side. Joseph repeatedly noticed the "Presence of God" and the Anointing that was on his life and the results he experienced because of the Anointing. Being beat by his brothers and left for dead couldn't stop him; being sold into slavery couldn't stop him; neither being put in prison for a crime he did not commit couldn't stop him.

You may or may not have been through what Joseph went through. Still the fact remains that we can get through any adversity that comes our way, we can out live anything.

We all have triumphs, of course, most are different small or large but they are still triumphs. Triumphs mean different things to different people no matter how great or insufficient it may seem. My Dad once told me, "We are to not discredit a person(s) effort if you really don't know why they are doing a specific thing."

At the least, we may be able to learn from what someone is doing or done and could possibly use it on our own situation. My sensitivity to be observant constantly increases and teaches me what right thing to do or what not to do. I heard someone say that, seventy percent or more of our learning comes from us observing or focusing on what we see.

Knowing and living out our purpose is the primary reason God birthed us into the earth. The fact is that He would not have brought us here without first knowing or revealing His assignment to us. And our purpose is highly significant and highly profitable. Our purpose is bigger than our mistakes our purpose is bigger than any sin. If the truth be told, before there was sin there was the birth of humanity and that first birth God had given purpose.

Someone maybe saying that, "I'm in my purpose because I live in a six figure house with more than one car." Or you may have all the cars and the house paid in full. We have to understand whatever God does is so big our finite thinking cannot comprehend it all. The fact is if our purpose is just for our immediate family and we are not being a blessing to multitudes then we might want to take our purpose to the next level. Or maybe we need to reevaluate our efforts that we call our purpose.

God has put something so massive and so lucrative in all of us it will be more than enough for generations to come in our family. In Proverbs 13:22 says, "A good man leaveth an inheritance to his children's children:" so would it be safe to say that our inheritance comes out of our purpose?

People for years have had questions about what they are supposed to be doing in life. I've heard these questions from people who have degrees in education and even people who seem to be doing well in their profession. No wonder college education debt is shooting through the roof, because people are in search their purpose or craft and they have no idea where to find it.

Please understand we will need the education system and possibly the job market to assist us with our purpose. However, "Seeking God First" for ourselves and especially for our children will send us down the right path and we'll pick up the necessary tools along the way. Matthew 6:33

How many times have we heard of someone working in a different field from what they studied in school? We as believers are chasing after money instead of, applying Kingdom Principles, and letting money chasing after us. That is a good indication that we are operating in our purpose.

Now there's nothing wrong with passing out flyers or business cards and going from door to door, however, this will only limit our results. If the truth be told, ninety to ninety-five percent of people throw away flyers and business cards in this twenty first century. So now we are depending on or putting pressure on the five to ten percent to generate profit for us.

When we resort on getting a website that go after the millions of people on a daily basis that genuinely admire and appreciate what we do and our efforts/purpose becomes multiple corporations established in the earth for God which aids and gives supply to multitudes. That's the kind of Kingdom Abundance God wants to produce through us.

God could very well want us to own the company or companies who we work for. But, how can that come to pass if we have a negative and complaining attitude for our employer? And, we find ourselves doing all the wrong things and never bringing anything to the table to better our work place. Let's face it we wouldn't give people like that a raise, promotion, or recognition. So, why should we expect to get a raise, promotion, or recognition if we have this type of attitude?

When I was growing up, countless times I would hear young adults say, "I'm going out into the world and find myself." Only if they knew that, our identity is not in this world however we shape this world through our identity and the standards or culture we set in our communities.

Just think about it everything we see today is a result of someone inventing, creating, or establishing something. But most importantly it all came out of The Mind or The Heart of God just to benefit us in this life.

So this creation or possibly a masterpiece came out of someone's intellect. And when they patent it or put their trademark on it, duplication is against the law which is simply saying go get your own creation and leave mine alone.

Or course, we know that a technique makes the difference on the success or down fall of our endeavors. For all of the many hamburger restaurants we have and all of them are successful the same is true for restaurants who sale chicken, steaks, seafood, and the list goes on.

The big differences these restaurants have are their techniques one of these business owners decided to offer something that the other owners were not offering. God has unlimited treasures and creations and He put some of this in us we just need to find out which one we are suppose to operate in.

Now, whenever you hear of this product, invention, or discovery we connect it to this person(s) because of the identity or the trademark they put into it. The real reason why they perfected it is because this became their passion and they took it as their lifelong assignment and making the necessary adjustments along the way. By that being the case, measurement of time or various challenges does not alter or discourage our persistence, therefore levels of progression is my daily objective.

Our purpose may have many identities because we will discover that we are good at more than one thing. Even when we were in elementary school we learned Math, English, and History and passed these courses and went on to pass even harder courses in high school and college. This is a sense of using our multiple talents to develop our various individual identities. And if the truth be told, we limit our intelligence if we think we are only good at one thing.

By stepping out of the box of "small thinking" and not depending on our "peanut ideas" our horizons will become many and our potentials will get us there.

God has put in us endless potential, aspirations, and achievements; when we tap into His Plan for our life through His Word. Then our daily reward will be successful achievements which will be a common and continuous lifestyle.

This is a principle that will work for anyone who will get involve. Massive dreams come true; witty ideas materialize; and lifelong solutions are an every day accomplishments for people who take off the limits.

If we associate ourselves with people who don't dream or think beyond their present potential, then we will find ourselves just trying to get from one day to the next with a "ball and chain" of struggles and setbacks.

God has placed me with Men and Women of God where I'm forced, just by association that takes me from levels to levels. I have become very observant, and I study and pay close attention to certain details in their life.

For instance focusing on the many situations they were confronted with and how they came through. Then finding out that the origin of their success or accomplishments was from God's Word. Then I understood this is not a secret that is kept from me neither did I have to pay hundreds or thousands of dollars for a course. I noticed I began to develop a spirit of persistence; not making the same mistake twice; and kept asking myself, "What can I do today that can take me closer to the place called there?"

We shouldn't just sit with our arms folded and expect for this vast revelation to fall into our laps. The only place where we will find success before work is in the dictionary. It may take many attempts at our vocation(s) before we realize our potential. It's been said that, "The only man who never makes a mistake is the man who never does anything."

I have personally be involved in many different job titles and the funny thing about it I enjoyed the different jobs and I did them very well. Also my efforts were recognize with awards, raises, and promotions. It wasn't long before I could be depended upon and trusted to do the most difficult tasks and many times I became a successful problem solver.

I love numbers I can memorize license plate just at one glance once I see a number or write it down I have it locked into my memory bank. So math and accounting procedures became easy for me sometimes working it out in my head without pencil and paper.

I remember times in elementary school I would come up with answers to math problems and couldn't explain how I did it. I love working with my hands in the areas of mechanicals, carpentry, and electrical. One of my goals is to bring these gifts to unlimited potentials.

During my times in elementary school, high school, and my short time in college I really didn't like reading or even writing. But I've always been good with expressing myself with words. Now figure that, I'm good with words but didn't like reading or writing. Hmm?

However as I began to spend time with God in worship and meditating on His Word I developed a love for reading and that lead me into writing. Little did I know that this process was the beginning of something powerful that God was trying to bring out in my life.

Keep in mind that my diligence in my job performances; my initiative for excellence and order (simply making better adjustments in the workplace) my knowledge from college education; and with my various job experiences played a big part into me getting to this present point.

As parents we have a highly important responsibility to notice our children in the area of intelligence. By paying close attention to their aspirations and their strong interest in something that may not be sensible, but to them they won't let it go and they become effortlessly good at it.

Take for instance if we notice our child likes to take things apart and see what's inside and see how it operates then put it back together. To me a light would come on for me and I would say; mechanics, electronics, or even carpentry. Or do we sometimes scold the child for taking an hundred dollar toy apart and severely punish them for this action. Or think of it as my hundred dollar investment now could bring us unlimited millions when this child comes up with witty inventions and solutions.

How many times have we heard of people taking college courses that seem to have nothing to do with their vocation, profession or even their passion? Now they spend the next twenty to thirty years doing something they totally hate. But because so much time and money was spent on their education they would not dare walk away from it. When they walk into their purpose they seem to blossom over night effortlessly and not allowing obstacles to distract them.

When I was growing up I was given two goals while in school get a good grade that was goal number one. Goal number two was to get a good paying job so I could support my family.

Someone maybe asking, "Who's at fault when my parents did not directly assist me into my purpose?" No one is to blame my parents did the best they knew how. My Mom was borne in the nineteen thirty's and she is the third oldest of sixteen children and she changed just as many diapers and prepared just as many meals as her Mom. My Dad was borne in the year of nineteen twenty eight raised on a farm and never went pass the fourth grade. So, allow me to ask, who is the blame?

God knew what kind of attitude and experiences it would take for me to effectively write. Some of the experiences I didn't like or even understood however it has been a piece by piece process molded together to produce results. I couldn't be the type of person to easily quit or let obstacles discourage me. I have become very selective who I share my aspirations with because everybody does not want you to be successful even family members.

As God would reveal the big picture to me with details and the necessary steps needed this would cause me to press on because of the objective and not the objects, which sometimes can be smoke screens designed to get us of course. To me the excitement would be so overwhelming sometimes all I could do is breakdown with tears of gratitude that He would entrust me with such a responsibility.

This also tells me that I must've passed the necessary tests to get to this point. And looking back it was worth all the tears of pain; it was worth all the disappointments; it was worth all the adjustments or corrections that I had to go through.

We must realize that our progression is an endless process once we reach a certain level God is saying, "Come Higher." In Psalm 115:14 says, "The Lord shall increase you more and more, you and your children." So it sound to me that if I stay in my process of progression my increase or success is unlimited. I have control of the amount of increase that I will receive according to my level of diligence to the process.

God has graced each and every one of us for a particular task. The dictionary describes "grace" as being, 1) A power coming from God that enables one to achieve such a state; 2) Any divine favor.

Simply put the "grace" we have to carry out a certain task this task becomes our passion and our passion becomes our wealth. We will not prosper in something that we are not passionate about. Our passion will always give us a solution when challenges arise, sometimes the challenge may be a sign to do something differently so we can get different or better results. This attitude is part of what it takes to move to the next level(s) and God will put people in our path to assist us with our vision.

Family please understand, that when God calls you out to do an assignment this is The Greatest opportunity and The Greatest calling known on earth. High above any political office; High above any CEO position; or High above any judicial position! So if we say that God has called us to do something and it seems to be a struggle to get off the ground it could be that our timing or technique might be off. We may not know enough about this task yet to fully step out.

Just like when Peter step out on the water he knew enough, or had enough faith, to get him out there and he stayed afloat for a short time. One thing he did not know that he couldn't pay attention to the different elements that were present and those elements became a distraction and he sank. Once he realize that he was out there because of what Jesus said then he put his focus back on Jesus then his faith increased and he began to walk on the water again Matthew 14:22-33. Peter's timing was right and his technique was right but he did not know enough to stay afloat. He lost focus on what got him out there simply by believing in The Word he got from Jesus.

How many times have we set out to do something with a Word from God? And things are going good with permanent progress then we find ourselves backing off of the things of God. Our meditation times become less or nonexistent or our church attendance decreases even our time in The Bible stops. Now we start focusing on and finding fault with things around us and the profit on our progress start drying up when before things were going smooth and now it seems to be a struggle just to do the simple things. Just do what Peter did and reach out for Jesus and He is more than able to get us back on course.

Another scenario that we can also relate to, is when we realistically look at someone who has been on their job for ten, fifteen, and twenty years and when they retire. What is it do they have to show for all the years of service? Small amounts of money in the bank or receive a retirement checks every month, or, of course, social security benefits.

Again Family, please understand God blesses us with abundance for us to bless others. There isn't any abundance in retirement or social security checks it's just enough to keep us broke. However if we are entitled for these benefits by all means take advantage of them but don't allow these benefits to be our primary source of finances. If these checks were to stop it would put us in a financial crisis with us seeking other ways to get out from under the pressure.

When we are purpose driven those benefits will be like crumbs, and depending on the economic status those benefits could dry up. But our purpose is saying I got you! Because with our purpose comes multiple streams of income and they keep multiplying upon multiplying.

Now understand, during their time of service, in the job market, before retirement they may have put their children through college or maybe paid off their house mortgage(s). However what they failed to realize that the skills and abilities that they have acquired over the years could have been tools or vehicles to fulfill their God given purpose.

Seems to me, if a person has retired from working I would think there could have been something during that time that would have opened the door to their purpose. Maybe aspirations of going in business for them self would have sprang up unless they found negative ways to decide against it. At this point it's not about me anymore but what I can leave to my children and grandchildren as an inheritance to keep them from struggling like I had to struggle. That's just pure selfishness, narrow mindedness, and fear of not wanting to accept the challenges that comes with success.

So, not knowing this they may live another twenty years and not even attempting or maybe not made aware that their purpose went beyond or included their livelihood, what a sad way to end a life. Keep in mind that this mindset has been extended into the children and maybe the grand children. Until someone realizes this is not the real way of life and they begin to see life from God's Perspective.

Now this person begins to walk in the things of God and be persistent in the things of God. So, this person begins to lead The Family into their God given purpose because The Family sees this person walking in his God given purpose. Now this Family becomes a beacon in the earth blessing others and fulfilling our God Given Purpose.

I am that person who will lead our Family out of the grips of not knowing our purpose. I accept the call I receive the challenge!

Think about it, Jesus took twelve men and none of them had The Holy Ghost and in three years made an impact on the entire world and this impact is still affecting mankind today and all they had was The Spoken Word from God and The Anointing on Jesus' Life.

Now, we have The Holy Spirit, The Written and Spoken Word of God, The Covenant of Abraham, plus the Bible says all we need is two or three agreeing to make a difference Matthew 18:19-20.

Sounds like to me that two or three of us can at least impact a city or even a state for God. All we need to do is learn to practice out our true citizenship of our true homeland which is "Heaven" and dominate with our "Kingdom Authority" through "God's Word." Of course we have a select few who are making many and large impacts on this world's system with "God's Word." Just think how much more effective we can be if we were all making the same impact as a body instead of individually.

If the truth just be told, we have the answers and the method to gain an abundance of resources to fulfill our purpose. To the believer the earth is just a big warehouse and by faith we have the ability to go to the shelves and get whatever we need.

Time after time again Jesus practiced His Kingdom Principles He did it whenever He wanted abundance He would call it forth; Matthew chapter 14 speaks of Jesus feeding the multitude with five loaves and two fish; Again in Matthew 17:27 Jesus called for money to come out of the mouth of a fish; Also in St. John 21:6 Jesus spoke multitude of fish into their nets.

However, when we as The Body of Christ follow through with our purpose we will be able to aid to a need out of our abundance and speak life and abundance into the lives of others. This is an individual effort channeled for collective results. In Proverbs 29:2 strongly states that, "When the righteous are in authority, the people rejoice:" now when I'm in position I gain authority and my authority is part of my purpose. Because without authority no purpose is effective or can be carried out properly; my authority will carry me into areas where I can exercise my purpose, this is just another form of dominance.

It's all about me bringing my purpose back to the Kingdom's table and join forces with other Kingdom Believers, so we can be more effective on destroying darkness also getting back to establish Godly Standards in our homes, in our society, and keeping The Church strong.

The Church is God's Kingdom here on earth that He established through Jesus and The Holy Spirit. Without God's Church on this earth it would be like a second hell with no laws, morals, or standards. We, The Church are the only reason God hasn't destroyed the earth and started over like in the days of Noah. And that is why Jesus is seated on the right hand of The Father interceding on our behalf to The Father because of His Love for The Church and His Love for Mankind.

God only knows Righteousness and The Purity of Righteousness God's thinking cannot comprehend anything less. However, Jesus says, "Father I was down there; I can understand some of their ignorance some of that ignorance was among My Disciples. Jesus is saying, "Father I'm raising up Men and Women of God who display The Kingdom Culture and people are starting to catch on." And The Father says, "Ok Jesus I'll hold off just because of Our Church and Our Passion for them."

All I'm saying Family, is that we have a "Serious Mission" and the urgency level is at an all time high. People are dying even at this very moment that needs what we have or need what we know. And that's why The Father is so bothered, when we being in The Body of Christ we have all the answers and solutions and people are dying in countless numbers daily not knowing what we know. And I have the nerve to get angry and take offence with someone because they didn't say good morning to me. How stupid is that?

Chapter 9

WE HAVE A DESTINY / COVENANT

As we see in the previous chapter of "What Is My Purpose" I mention multiple developments come out of our purpose. At some point and time, this development removes the limits that we sometimes place on ourselves. This may cause us to be an alone pioneer in our quest, which is fine, because very few if any will think the same way we do when we set our horizons for unusual accomplishments.

Purpose is so important concerning our Destiny; our designed purpose will keep us on the right path of our Destiny.

Our true God given Destiny is not something that dies, understand God's Plan will be fulfilled in the earth rather through us or through someone else. When this life has expired for us then our Destiny becomes a legacy or Covenant and someone will be in place to continue with it.

I'm sure we all have noticed in the business world when the father of a corporation becomes successful. Then his age has a way of not allowing him to make profitable decisions any longer or his death has left his position vacant. We have seen his children boy or girl take this corporation(s) to levels that fit their growth and become more profitable.

Just like with The Covenant God made with Abraham, then it was passed on to Isaac, then Jacob picked it up and ran with it. Now we being the seed of Abraham and co-heirs with Christ Jesus we have a better Covenant that we must continue with.

CHAPTER 10

GOD GIVES US "STEWARDSHIP AND INTEGRITY"

The next level which will bring us increase is "stewardship" and "integrity" which is also a way of life channeled through our mindset. Rather we realize it or not we practice "stewardship" and "integrity" on some level on a daily basis in areas of our life. Some people are more intense with it than others which happen to explain why some receive more than others. Order with Excellence and Stewardship which is when Integrity has to surface and be the ultimate in organized living.

This is a guaranteed way to keep increase flowing in areas of our lives; we'll be presented with opportunities; we'll find ourselves in positions of authority; influential people will begin to rely on us; of course we'll have favor, and the list goes on.

Some definitions of "stewardship" is (a) the office, duties, and obligations of a steward. (b) the conducting, supervising, or managing of something; especially: the careful and responsible management of something entrusted to one's care.

Defining "steward" means (a) someone who protects or is responsible for money, property, etc. (b) a person whose job is to manage the land and property of another person.

A definition of "integrity" (a) uprightness of character; honesty (b) unimpaired state; soundness (c) undivided or unbroken state; completeness.

So we see that "stewardship" is merely the act or obligation of being a "good steward." And because we practice "stewardship" this allows "integrity" to surface and we habitually do the right thing even if no one is watching. Again this not something that we pick up or lay it down when it's convenient but this becomes a way of life and the benefits of it is unlimited.

In the Bible people who were "stewards" held offices such as preachers, teachers, elders, and bishops. Even though it's not mention "integrity" played a big part because trust and honesty had to be present in their lives. They also had their affairs in order and had acquired the mindset to be compassionate for other people's concerns and able to minister simple solutions from The Word of God. People representation and adhering to people's needs were their primary concern. Titus 1:7-9 Now, how can you acquire that kind of mindset without "stewardship" and "integrity?"

These people who were in authority and held offices spent a lot of time with God which saturated them with His Glory and for them to follow in His Truth on a daily basis. By doing this, they learned how to solve or eliminate certain life's issues through The Word of God and it valued them in their dealings with people. It's no question that God's Knowledge and Wisdom flowed in their lives continually because of how much they relied on God's Word. Every situation that we will ever be confronted with and every obstacle that may come our way can be solved by God's Word.

The Word of God has not lost power we sometimes falter in our trust, belief, or our faith which weakens the effect of what His Word is suppose to do. There is life in God's Word; There is an abundance of resources in God's Word; There is direction and answers in God's Word. However if we neglect to search God's Word for these powerful Treasures of Promises then life can be of little meaning and of little purpose.

This is just another part of our "stewardship" by searching the scriptures to apply the scriptures to our life daily. For "stewardship" to be effective in any area of our lives we must first be a good "stewardship" of God's Word. Because God's Word will begin to correct or affect areas of our life where change needs to happen. Then we will branch out into areas in our home; in our workplace; in our church activities; and of course in our relationships.

It's not going to be easy for some of us because we have been doing it our way for a long time and maybe all of our lives. If we were able to see into the future and realize how important this transformation is needed for us to adhere to we will begin to help family members; our co-workers;

our church family; and just society as a whole. We may not ever know who we will affect by what we do or say but one thing for sure if we are following Christ then it will not be a problem for people to follow us.

There are many areas of "stewardship" and "integrity" that some of us might not realize. But if you remember the definition being that we are to be trusted to look over or handle something that belongs to someone else. If we start with what might seem to be the minor things first and correct those then this will begin to attack other areas that need attention. Here are ways we can test ourselves in the area of "stewardship" and "integrity."

Take for instance, our jobs; do we sometimes clock in and out at the prescribed time? Or do we give weak excuses when we are found to be late or leave early? Have we been guilty of taking something as small as a paper clip or ink pen home with us? Let's face it we all have been guilty of this practice and found ways to justify it. Saying something like, "they don't pay me enough so they owe me this or they won't miss it because they have so much."

Please understand, that one item will be multiplied times the people who do and also by the many times we may take that item. Most times those people, who take these items, are the first to complain about not getting a raise. When upper management in the company is realizing the cost of supplies keep going up instead of down. So they (upper management) feel why should we give employee raises when supply cost is not going down? We also need to realize that owners, managers, and supervisors, most times, were in the shoes of the hourly employees so they know what is going on.

I've been out in public and went into restrooms where the water was left running in the sink and unused paper towels on the floor. "Integrity" says pick up the paper towels and turn off the running water and I do it. Come on people we can learn to employ "integrity" on a small level so it can have a snowball effect to bigger savings that will benefit "US." And because of the savings that will finally surface in supply cost we could see more raises on our jobs.

What if the employees get together and attack these areas and begin to correct them? Then maybe a year goes by and upper management recognizes a twenty percent decline in supply cost. Now they have the opportunity to give hourly employees permanent increases because of the hard work they did to avoid waste. It won't happen over night and it may take longer than a few months, but someone must eventually see the big picture and start the process. It'll be fewer lay-offs practically no terminations and the hiring cycle doesn't become or remain a revolving door. It's up to lower management and hourly employees to make this attack effective and profitable.

My "integrity" is constantly looking for ways to better save resources in my workplace, at home, at church or just in the general public. For instance, if I'm home alone I don't need every light to be turned on in the house just one or two lights on in the room that I am in is enough. When leaving from a small restroom turn the light and water off and try to use fewer paper towels.

A shopping example; when we are in the Supermarket and get something off the shelf and put it our shopping cart with the intention of paying for it. Then before we get to the check out we decide we don't need that item and put it back on the shelf out of place.

When "integrity" is saying take that item back to where we got it from and put it in the proper place. Or how many times after unloading our bags into the car and we leave the shopping cart in the middle of the parking lot? Again "integrity" is saying take the shopping cart back into the store for someone else to use. Or now they have designated areas in the parking lot to retrieve shopping carts. Why not at least take the cart to these areas?

Now these stores have to hire someone just to place items back into their proper place. Just like with the shopping cart, people have to get hired to retrieve shopping carts from all over the parking lot. Where do you think the money comes from to pay these extra employees salaries? From us, when prices go up on stores items we are the first to complain that prices have went up. Someone might be saying that this is just one item or one shopping cart and you might be right.

Again, when you multiply that item or that shopping cart times the number of people who do it. It turns into a full time job for someone just to keep up. Plus someone could be watching our act of "integrity" and they decide to take that item back to the proper place or even take the shopping cart back to the prescribed area. They may imitate our act of "integrity" and stick to it and they may not ever realize how important this is and it can start a "snowball effect" and cause others to reap benefits in their lives.

Again, we all have been guilty of doing these things, however, if we want to experience levels of Kingdom Living. Then we must employ Kingdom Principles daily in our lives for the rest of our lives, it's all in The Bible. These Principles are not hidden from us neither is it difficult to understand.

Another quick example is, when we stay in Hotels and take the towels, shampoo, or soap that we don't use. We try and justify it by saying, "I paid for this room so I'm entitled to take these extra items." So, the cost of Hotel supplies go up and, you guessed it, so does the price of the room go up.

When we are out in the public and toss something into the trash and miss the can. Do we leave it on the ground or, does "integrity" tell us to pick it up and put it into the trash can? Again someone has to be hired to clean up the trash we refuse to put away properly. So, our taxes go up or the price of getting into certain public facilities or events increase.

The same is true in restaurants no matter what level of quality the restaurants displays. Do we sneak off extra condiments into our possession? Then when we go back to the same restaurant we find that the prices have increased, of course, there are many more examples. When it's tax time, how truthful have we been? When coupons say one per household, how many friends do we line up with those coupons?

The list may stop or continue depending on where you are in life and with your life style. The point I'm trying to make is we want God to bless us with increase. How can God trust us with increase when we keep taking from others every chance we get? Don't make the mistake with our level of "stewardship" and "integrity" and only apply them for certain things or in certain areas of our lives instead of applying "stewardship" and "integrity" in every aspect of our lives.

All of these practices are poor examples of "stewardship" and "integrity" and if not eliminated from our lives this poor behavior will lead to bigger takes because we have convinced ourselves that we are getting away with it. When in actuality we are making it worse for ourselves and when our children become involve with this behavior this could become a crisis and may involve law enforcement.

We really don't have to wait and go shopping, or go out to eat, or maybe go to a public event before we can employ "stewardship or integrity." We can start right here where we live. When was the last time we cleaned out that cluttered closet and constantly kept it neat and orderly? How about that junk drawer that we may have receipts two and three years old with a handful of pencils and pens? What about the basement or attic that has items that need to be thrown out? Do I need to mention the garage or the storage sheds that some of us have? Or maybe we need to rearrange our sock drawer or go in our clothes closet and rearrange the clothes we keep on hangers.

I try and keep my place that I live in clean, neat, and orderly at all times as if I was going to have company everyday. And sometimes weeks go by before people come over and that doesn't bother me at all.

The simple fact is, how can we employ "stewardship and integrity" away from the home when it's not used in the home? Then we wonder why we get overlooked when it comes to promotions and raises.

As we go into these areas and make these small changes things will become easier to maintain. We will also find that "integrity" covers a wide range of things; from our hygiene to our way of cooking; to the way we take care of our vehicles; to how we perform in our workplace; to how we dress neatly with superior grooming standards.

Again someone might be saying, "This "integrity" thing is a lot and the list is long." To the person who is saying this, you are right however look how long we have been doing it this way.

My question would be, "When will change start?" Will we have to wait another twenty, thirty, or fifty years with little or no results and wonder why things aren't getting any better? We cannot expect to do the same thing and get different results. Simply put, that's insanity.

Someone might be saying, "I haven't done any of this and I have everything in order, or it seems that way, and I still don't have increase I'm just living from pay check to pay check.

It may be that you might need to go to God and lay it all on line with Him. For instance, "Father I know Your Word says this and I'm doing this, and I know Your Word says that and I'm doing that. Please Holy Spirit show me what else I need to do to have my increase or harvest released to me." Saying something like that earnestly that'll get Heavens attention and the blockage will be revealed to us. Remember The Father wants to give us our abundance more than we want to have it.

Here's another point we might want to consider. What are we doing to help someone else to increase on a continuous basis? When was the last time we volunteered our services on someone else's project? When was the last time we took someone to lunch or dinner, or maybe just bought someone a soft drink or a cup of coffee? With a heart of gratitude! So, God is saying, "Why should I increase you when you have not allowed increase to come in anyone else's life?"

In Galatians 6:7 "...for whatsoever a man soweth, that shall he also reap." So, it's safe to say if we are sowing (giving) "poor practices of stewardship" when no one gains from our efforts then there will be little or no gain in our life. One of the ways to create a giving heart within yourself and get God's attention is to give in tithes and offering at the church that you attend.

In Malachi 3:10, "Bring all the tithes into the storehouse, (church) That there may be meat (ample sufficiency) in My House, And prove Me (do this principle continuously) now in this, Says the Lord of host, If I will not open for you the windows of Heaven and pour out for you a blessing that there will not be room enough to receive it."

Just think about it, if we are in position and doing the Word because of the love we have for The Father. What benefit would it be for the Father to keep our increase He doesn't need it He created it for us to have. When He sees us rejoicing with our increase He rejoices. The enemy is also defeated through our "Praise to The Father" that could be the answer right there. Are we praising Him and Thanking Him for what He has already done with a loving heart of gratitude for what He's about to do?

Praise takes our mind off of the situation and puts our mind on God's Promises. So, the next time the enemy brings us a picture of a bad situation, we give him a good picture of "Praises and Confessing God's Promises." Amen?

Believe it or not that makes a big difference on when and how much we receive from God. Just think about it, we like giving to people who say nice things about us. God is the same way and as we love on The Father in Praise and Worship we acquire favor with our Father God.

CHAPTER 11

GOD GIVES US HIS CHARACTER

Let's start out in the beginning when God created man we will began to open everything up after these scriptures. Genesis 1:26-28, God said, "Let Us make man in Our image, according to Our likeness; let them have dominion over the fish of the sea, over the birds of the air, and over the cattle, over all the earth and every creeping thing that creeps on the earth."

So God created man in His own image; in the image of God He created him; male and female He created them.

Then God blessed them, and God said to them, "Be fruitful and multiply; fill the earth and subdue it;

As we look at the Awesomeness of God His mental capacity cannot be limited nor will we ever understand His infinite thinking. Even at that, He did not want us to limit ourselves in our mental capacities and through His Power we can do all things.

What I mean when I say not to limit our mental capacities is simply this, do not enter a situation and think it will defeat you. Set goals after goals don't just stop with a few accomplishments but let us keep going until we finish our course and completed our destiny. In 2 Timothy 4:7 The Apostle Paul says, "I have fought a good fight, I have finished my course, I have kept the faith:"

We have to make it because it paves the way for others to make it this thing is much bigger than us. Some people may not think they can't have goals and achieve them until they see us achieving our goals. We are clearly a product of our own thoughts and decisions. Where we are going is determined by our environmental influences, namely friends and family. It's good to associate with the kind of people who are going in a positive and Godly direction.

If you look closely at the different things God has provided for us to control. All if not most has been establish in our school system and considered part of our education. The study of animals, sea life, live stock, and insects is a major part in developing our culture in all parts of the world.

Man has made millions upon millions of livelihood dollars investigating this powerful knowledge. Just think about it we pay schools for their courses and books to study this material and then go on and make a profession of it because of these studies. This is a good thing, no way is it bad as long as it remains in the guidelines for what God has created it to become.

Understand that all of the knowledge we have gained in these many areas came out of God. Not to say the least which is a very small part of who He is. When you look at all of the profitable ways of life in our society, the core of it came out of God first. This is what Adam had discovered in the Garden of Eden unlimited knowledge, strength, and resources.

Everything we need is in the earth for us to survive and prosper there has not been nor will it ever be a shortage of resources on this earth. It all depends on who or where we are getting our information from and who or what we're relying on for our resources.

Do we want just enough for me and mine to get by on or do we want it until it over flows? Once again, God says, "He gives us life abundantly (to the full, till it over flows)" St. John 10:10 AMP. That doesn't sound like a shortage to me! Again we stop or start that process by what we are saying or by the way we think. We will not be able to receive something different than what we are saying or thinking.

Someone may be saying, "I don't want all that abundance neither do I believe in it." When we qualify for God's abundance, He gives it to us for one reason and that is to bless others so others can bless others. Our only purpose in life is for people, just like Jesus, everything Jesus did was for the benefit of people.

When I look and see the many profitable businesses and the many mega churches God has raised up. One day I said, "Where do I fit in with all of this?" There are multiple things I love to do and good at it.

My first initial love for writing came about ten to twelve years ago. I would just copy verses out of the Bible and pray them over my life and the lives of people I was connected to. From that I developed more of a love to write prayers, I think that became the ultimate inspiration. I could just sit down and meditate or search the scriptures and began to speak to the situation or speak into a person(s) life on paper.

I began to pass out these prayers to different individuals who were interested. To this day I still pray scriptures over myself, family members, and friends. The more I do it the more the scriptures become real, alive, and become manifested into what The Word said was going to happen. Sometimes I go back and read some of my early prayers and the "Anointing" is still flowing out of these words. Sometimes tears flow and sometimes more revelation flows out of me, or maybe both.

Of course, I didn't realize this kind of love for writing would ever reach this magnitude of putting what I'm saying in books. One thing for sure, if I didn't allow God to change my life, no message would be given or a profitable word could be spoken. The "Anointing" in these words would not remove burdens and destroy yokes in the lives of people who read this book.

I once heard a statement said, "Whatever it is that you are good at and it's easy for you to do, that is your ticket." Meaning, this is the thing that God has put inside of us so we can be anointed to bless other people. Another statement was once said, "We're to have multiple streams of income." This is one of the characteristics of God He supplies many things at the same time so it leads me to believe we are to be good at doing more than one thing.

There's a perfect example of some men who were profitable and the one who was not in Matthew 25:15-29 that says,

And unto one he gave five talents (money), to another two, and to another one; to every man according to his several (many) ability; and straightway took his journey.

Then he that had received the five talents went and traded with the same, and made them other five talents.

And likewise he that had received two, he also gained other two.

But he that had received one went and digged in the earth, and hid his lord's money.

After a long time the lord of those servants cometh, and reckoned with them.

And so he that had received five talents came and brought other five talents, saying, Lord, thou deliveredst unto me five talents: behold, I have gained beside them five talents more.

His lord said unto him, Well done, thou good and faithful servant: thou hast been faithful over a few things, I will make thee ruler over many things: enter thou into the joy of the lord.

He also that had received two talents came and said, Lord, thou deliveredst unto me two talents: behold, I have gained two other talents beside them.

His lord said unto him, Well done, thou good and faithful servant; thou hast been faithful over a few things, I will make thee ruler over many things: enter thou into the joy of thy lord.

Then he which had received the one talent came and said, Lord, I knew thee that thou art an hard man, reaping where thou hast not sown, and gathering where thou hast not strawed:

And I was afraid, and went and hid thy talent in the earth: lo, there thou hast that is thine.

His lord answered and said unto him, Thou wicked and slothful servant, thou knewest that I reap where I sowed not, and gather where I have not strawed:

Thou oughtest therefore to have put my money to the exchangers (bank), and then at my coming I should have received mine own with usury (interest).

Take therefore the talent from him, and give it unto him which hath ten talents.

For unto every one that hath shall be given, and he shall have abundance: but from him that hath not shall be taken away even that which he hath.

As we see with the man who had the one talent he was afraid so he did nothing with his talent. However his talent is as valuable as the other men who had their talents but he chose to do nothing with it. So as it happen he lost what he had and it was given to the man who was profitable and not afraid.

How many times have we heard people say they need money for this or they need money for that, and when they get a piece of money they don't do right by it. Most times they spend the money on the wrong thing and expect God to bail them out of their dilemma. I can't began to tell the many times I did this very thing and God told me, "I gave you the money for that already" but because I mishandled the money. I expected God to rush and bail me out again and again. Until I had to learn just pay close attention on how I was handling my affairs and get Him involved in my decisions of what I should do with the money. God loves when we get Him involved in our affairs and He waits for an entry to put His Hand in our situation.

CHAPTER 12

GOD GIVES US HIS CREATION, THE EARTH

Everything that we see in the natural first came from the "Spirit" or commonly known as "The Spirit of God." When He spoke everything into existence in Genesis chapter one, His Words developed, shape, and created all that we have today. He even foreseen all of the inventions that we came up with and there are more inventions to come.

This earth is complete with all resources enough to supply the millions and billions of people on planet earth. What kind of God would we have if He allowed the existence of man-kind and did not supply us with all the necessary things that it takes for us to live in abundance?

Have you ever took the time and look at the many beautiful mountains that God created for us. These mountains now have names; man has made a sport out of climbing them, or just simply made luxurious resorts out of these enormous Creations.

The thousands and millions of acres of forest trees that we have and able to perform studies or hunt wild-life. Valleys designed where we could have communities, towns, and cities. The many caves hold history of human and animal life; canyons which we enjoy and even made famous exhibits of.

The many seas, rivers, lakes, the small streams and brooks it's been recorded that three fourths of the earth is covered with water yet enough land to accommodate billions of people. Man couldn't do that, only God Our Father could make such a land to last for generations upon generations.

There are still millions of acres all over the world of undeveloped land. I can only believe that there is still abundance of resources in this undeveloped land. There is a large amount of undeveloped land preserved for our wild-life. Just as it is with the rivers, seas, and lakes included with all the sea life, let's face it they (the animals) are here to live also. God intended for us to have plenty of resources for our living needs and for our livelihood.

As you have seen we have taken each part of God's Creation and made professions of them; studying of wild-life never ends; it seems new species are constantly being found in our waters; and of course, the forest and the ground itself has given us wood, paper, metals, iron, plastics, and the different fabrics we use to make our clothes.

Again, we must understand that everything man has ever done or will ever do was first birthed out of The Spirit of God and The Mind of God. Everything good that has ever entered into the earth came through God first. That is, before sin contaminated and distorted the original purpose of what God had intended for His Creation to be.

Let's look at The Garden of Eden, it's been recorded that the architectural plans for Eden provided homes and abundant land for living for one million human beings. At the *narrowest* point of entrance into The Garden of Eden was only twenty-seven miles wide. In the beginning it seldom rained in Eden; however each night because of the artificial irrigation channels, a mist would go up to refresh the vegetation of The Garden.

As confirmation to these historical findings Genesis 2:5-9 AMP;

When no plant of the field was yet in the earth and no herb of the field had sprung up, for the Lord God had not [yet] caused it to rain upon the earth and there was no man to till the ground,

But there went up a mist (fog, vapor) from the land and watered the whole surface of the ground

And the Lord God formed man of the dust of the ground, and breathed into his nostrils the breath *or* spirit of life, and man became a living being.

And the Lord God planted a garden toward the east, in Eden [delight]; and there He put the man whom He had formed (framed, constituted).

And out of the ground the Lord God made to grow every tree that is pleasant to the sight *or* to be desired good (suitable, pleasant) for food; the tree of life also in the center of the garden, and the tree of the knowledge of [the difference between] good and evil *and* blessing and calamity.

The Garden of Eden was of such great size that a river ran through it and it was divided into four parts, Genesis 2:10-15 AMP.

Now a river went out of Eden to water the garden; and from there it divided and became four [river] heads.

The first named Pishon; it is the one flowing around the whole land of Havilah, where there is gold.

The gold of that land is of high quality, bdellium (pearl?) and onyx stone are there.

The second river is named Gihon; it is the one flowing around the whole land of Cush.

The third river is named Hiddekel [the Tigris]; it is the one flowing east of Assyria. And the fourth river is the Euphrates.

And the Lord God took the man and put him in the Garden of Eden to tend and guard *and* keep it.

Someone might be saying, "What does all this have to do with the character of God?" One of the points that need to come out is God thinks on a much larger scale than we do. He looks at the whole package from beginning to end and we may find ourselves concentrating on the crumbs.

Time and time again, I would say, "God I need money for a certain necessity or for an emergency." But the Mind of God is saying, "I want and is trying to get you to a place where all your needs will be met forever." But we sometimes want a "quick financial fix" which can happen. However, the Mind of God wants us to know that "quick financial fixes" is not the ultimate place of security.

In some cases it may not be financial it could be healing from a sickness, marital problems, family pressures, or a job situation needs to change. God will handle that and more this is not a problem for God. At some point I can only believe The Holy Spirit is trying to nudge us, through God's Word, to a place where we walk in divine health; also that we may live in marital bliss; have harmonious families; and we operate our own successful businesses. The main objective of us being blessed and rising up so that we can bless others and show them how to rise up.

By spending time with God in His Word also in Praise and Worship on a daily basis it's an absolute guaranteed for results. His Word says, in Psalms 67:5-6, "Let the people praise Thee, O God; let all the people praise Thee."

"Then shall the earth yield her increase; and God, even our own God, shall bless us." Also in Psalms 85:11-12 says that, "Truth shall spring out of the earth; and righteousness shall look down from heaven."

"Yea, the Lord shall give that which is good; and our land shall yield her increase."

Sounds to me this is a complete package for a manifested harvest and all I have to do is get before God daily. Now say, "Wow!" I can do this! The fact is evident that praises and worshipping God gives us favor with Him. Amen? So come on Family let's get on board with this Kingdom Exercise! Again let's say, "Wow!" I can do this!

Plus by doing this, He will bring to our attention what is already on the inside of us and show us ways for these treasures to surface. God will begin to bring to our attention the thing we "enjoy" doing with little or no effort and getting maximum results and large compensations for our efforts.

The most important word in the previous statement is "enjoy" we cannot omit this essential element. The simple fact remains, is that if we do not "enjoy" what we are doing. We will become easily discouraged, sidetracked, or lose focus there will be little or no progress because we will always look for shortcuts. Which will make our efforts look useless and eventually we will not be able carry out the demands that the position is calling for. We won't have unction to learn better methods, or even go higher in our education so we can gain supervisory skills that put us in position(s) of authority.

However, if we enjoy what we are doing then we will diligently find ways to work through discouragement, disappointments, or even set backs. Failure is not a reason to quit, but only a reason to find different methods that will be more productive in what we are trying to do. We need to understand that failure could sometimes be something trying to get our attention to go a different route. All because we are "enjoying" what we are doing, this keeps us always looking for ways to take it to more productive levels. People who we are associated with us during this endeavor, they become inspired because of our enthusiasm and energy and they will start to give positive input that will get us through varies challenges a lot easier, because challenges will come.

Of course we know this does not come by just sitting around and waiting for it to fall in our laps. We may start out doing something we don't entirely like or agree with. But, the fact still remains we need to be active in doing something because we understand "stewardship" and "integrity" and now know how to give an honest day's work. God will recognize and honor our diligence and He will begin to open doors for our advancements and promotions.

Just like earlier in this chapter when I brought up Matthew 25:15-29 where it speaks of the three guys with the different talents (or different amounts of money). The guy who was diligent and found ways to double his earnings he was rewarded with even more talents. But to the guy who did nothing with what he had, because it was little but not insignificant, lost what he had and suffered remorse and tragedy.

It may be that someone might be working a job that's paying minimum wage. If you work that job honestly and diligently promotion is guaranteed it doesn't matter who likes you or not and it may not happen over night. For the simple fact that you are working God's Principles you will not be denied or overlooked. Now you'll begin to see how to handle more increase because you have been faithful in handling the little.

Now as you continue to experience advancements and increase because of the Godly Principles that you operate on a daily basis. The Holy Spirit will begin to open your eyes and you'll see things that you've never seen before. Some of the things The Holy Spirit will show you are the things that have been there all the time. And because we are thinking clearly and can see things through the eyes of The Holy Spirit. We will begin to operate in areas we didn't think would be possible.

As we follow through with this process and begin to conquer bigger, and what seems to be, more difficult challenges we will start to develop an attitude that winning is our only and absolute result or way out. Defeat is not entertained nor is it an option.

One thing for sure there is always an answer and a positive solution to any situation. And in our case we are anointed and empowered to get Godly results which always gives increase. The application might be different depending on the situation but the method of positivity and optimism remains the same which is where our faith in God's Word has to be our final and only step.

We have to understand that the answer is always on the inside of us at all times. Sometimes we tend to lean away from the availability of The Holy Spirit, of course when we allow this to take place things become extremely difficult. In 1 Corinthians 14:33 says, For God is not the author of confusion, but of Peace... Also in Matthew 11:30 states, For My yoke is easy, and My burdens is light. Matthew 11:30 (AMP) For My yoke is wholesome (useful, good-not harsh, hard, sharp, or pressing, but comfortable, gracious, and pleasant), and My burden is light and easy to be borne (or carry).

If we feel resistance or complications and we may not know what to do next first of all we need to invite The Peace of God to step in. Something as simple as getting off to a quiet place and meditate with The Holy Spirit asking Him for His direction. He will always reveal to us what is the correct and most effective thing to do and most times it's something simple. It may be we are having difficulty with someone; The Holy Spirit might say take this person to lunch (breakfast, dinner) and just show them some love. Or maybe having a problem with a creditor; again

The Holy Spirit might say, just keep making your monthly payments on time.

God is not difficult, but by using our act of obedience as an avenue to give Him entry to get involve. This difficult person that we are having issues with might end up becoming our best friend. Or, the creditor might decide to cancel our debt or at least give us favor or maybe decide to give their life to Christ because of the God they see in us. It's how we perceive a thing which will determine what kind of a result we will get.

I would like to focus in on the title of this book, "We Have The Kind of God Who *Gives*." First of all, I could never sum up the many things that God *Gives* a warehouse of books would not come close to describe His Massiveness. The Bible only gives us short "faith truths" of who He is and what He can do. As we grow with our walk with Him we find each day is different and no two moments are the same for billions of people all over the earth.

So, since God is so massive in His character and provisions. I have no other reason than to rely on His Word (which is perfect) as to channel me in ways that glorify Him and give me abundance in all areas of my life. I'm convinced and I pray by you reading this material you have been inspired to believe on Him because He already believes in us.

In 1 Timothy 4:14-16 AMP, Do not neglect the gift which is in you, [that special inward endowment] which was directly imparted to you [by The Holy Spirit]…

Practice *and* cultivate *and* meditate upon these duties; throw yourself wholly into them [as your ministry], so that your progress may be evident to everybody.

Look well to yourself [to your own personality] and to [your] teaching; persevere in these things [hold to them], for by so doing you will save both yourself and those who hear you.

CHAPTER 13

GOD GIVES US THE ENDLESS BEAUTY OF OUR WOMEN

Before woman came on the earth she was the last of God's creation. God spoke everything else into existence and through the help of Adam's work God prepared a lifestyle of complete abundance and graceful living for Eve to enter into.

God made Woman only for her to exhibit her true beauty and for His Treasures to surface in her life so to benefit the rest of humanity. I have to believe by her walking in this type of awesomeness portrays areas in her life that gives perfection.

God had everything prepared for her, And why not? Because, God didn't want her to experience anything missing or lacking He wanted everything to be complete for her. By this being the case, now her true identity of her beauty can surface and she can flow into her God given purpose.

Our Woman doesn't need to worry how the mortgage, electric bill, phone bill, internet, cable and how the car note is going to be paid.

Instead we as Men need to bring her into a debt-free home; driving debt-free cars and, we as men, working in our God Given Purpose which consistently brings in lucrative amounts of finances.

Because if they make gold toothpicks then my wife should have them; gold handled hair brushes; gold faucet handles; crystal and gold chandeliers, and etc. this is the least that my wife should have.

The title of Why not bring her above and take her beyond from where she is now in her living standards and when this is happening the more of her unlimited beauty surfaces, and now everybody benefits. What can be better than a smile and words of complimentary satisfaction coming from a woman who's excelling in her true identity.

I have to believe Adam's communing with God, of course, allowed him to acquire a relationship with The Father and prepared Adam for the entry of Eve and how to have a relationship with her. I'm sure God had started to impart into Adam things that he would need for their marriage or better known as "relationship/marital standards."

As we know, the animals took on different roles in caring for their young and their young took the nature or behavior of their parents and, of course, that way of life for the animals became repetitive.

God knew Adam had noticed this in the animals and I'm sure this was discussed between God and Adam. The truth is, Adam had no idea his was missing anything, I honestly believe, Adam thought this was it, his main objective was to work and please God. Just like we, as men, are to work and please our wives or at least be more diligent in pleasing our wives first, everything else second!

Our lives as the husband will be much easier if our wives know they remain first in our marriage. And not playing second fiddle to Mom and Dad, our children, our jobs and even putting her before our own needs. For instance; our vehicles; our love for sports; hanging out with the guys; or our little hobbies that take up large portions of our time.

We have to understand that we define our wives and our wives define us. They have qualities that benefit our character and we have qualities that benefit their character. Together we mold this into a unit (called the marriage) and become productive with our new found treasures. However our main reason for productivity is to be looked upon by others and they learn and profit from our accomplishments. Simply put, "we are blessed to be a blessing."

For those of us men who love studying The Word, we have to find balance and maybe include her in our studies. Maybe give each other Word Exercises that benefits growth in Word Knowledge and most of all Word applications. Believe it or not they (our wives) are loaded with revelations that are essential for the marriage and possibly for The Ministry we may be involved in.

By us as husbands we begin to use this method with our wives then this will start to awake the many hidden treasures of her true identity. And her true identity will surface into unlimited potentials. To say the least, she has understandings and mental angles that are specifically designed to benefit the Kingdom of God and to benefit the marriage because all of what is in our wives came out of The Heart of God and given to us (as husbands) to love and nurture her through The Word of God.

So, how can we as husbands make this happen for our wives if we are not awakening the treasures that remain in us? Is it safe to say, that my main objective before we receive our wives is to work on ourselves and allow these enormous potentials to surface.

Our main purpose in life is to spend time with God; hear God's Words; and obey His Commands that's it. This is the umbrella we are supposed to live by and under this produces everything else; our provision; our direction; our purpose; and our destiny. It doesn't take a rocket scientist or someone with many college degrees to understand this.

In the relationship Adam had with God, this allowed his enormous treasures to surface in his life. And what better way to learn first class relationship methods than directly from God Himself. God had saturated Adam's life off of His Spoken Word and today we lived off the written Word The Bible and Spoken Word of God.

Family please understand, at this point and time in creation Adam did not know sin. He survived off The Spoken Word of God daily he was an exact replica of God's Word. There was not any selfishness in Adam that had him wondering "what about me." He lived out every Word of God to the letter and not coming short in any area. Just like God did not come short with Adam and all that Adam needed in The Garden.

We have to understand that God created us to be progressive thinkers with an inquisitive nature and always bringing on new ideas; looking for better and more positive ways to do a thing; exploring different avenues of adventure which promotes endless learning.

How do we think travels in space came about and how we learn to survive in that type of atmosphere? One answer and that is, progressive thinking by exercising endless learning. How do we think fast cars can exceed two hundred miles per hour; and how bridges can hold millions of tons of traffic for decades? Again, progressive thinking! It's been said that a genius only uses ten percent of their brain. I glad I'm a genius what about you!

I have come to realize that we carry an unlimited supply of potential and intelligence. However we limit that supply through negative influences of our environment and a lack of continuous and aggressive learning. When we allow our learning to stop no matter what the age, life becomes a stand still with little or no purpose. Progression then becomes limited or just eliminated all together and we lead ourselves into areas of wrong choices and even sometimes rationalize the truth, which is a dangerous area.

Then we find that ignorance takes over through self deception and we have little or no progress, direction, purpose, or even goals. Hosea 4:6 states, "My people are destroyed for lack of knowledge..." In 2 Timothy 2:15 also states that we are to, "Study to show thyself approved unto God, a workman that needeth not to be ashamed, rightly dividing the word of truth.

We must understand knowledge is power and sometimes contains untruth as well as truth. When we cease to gain knowledge then we die, first the mind and then the body. When we get knowledge we need to decide if it's true or untrue then determine if it's beneficial for our mental development and growth.

Like all foods are not good for us, and we have to decide rather we will eat whatever is good or not good. I'm sure the picture is clear that we have to be mindful on what we take on as profitable knowledge or unprofitable knowledge. In either case profitable knowledge is a weapon against ignorance and nothing can penetrate or go beyond the Knowledge of God which is The Ultimate Power of Truth.

When we take our natural progressive knowledge of truth and allow God to put His Hand in the mix. Then we'll get better results than those anointed people in The Bible.

It's time to allow God to do a new thing in our lives at least this new thing that God wants to do is new to us. For instance when it might take some people, without God in their lives, a lifetime or many years to accomplish a thing then it might just take us weeks or months to accomplish the same task.

By now we can clearly see God was giving Adam knowledge and preparing Adam's mindset for Eve's entry. Adam's way of thinking was not to reflect animalistic ideas or thoughts. However, as he'd notice how the adult animals would care for their young and how the male figures are the strong forces in a family setting. This method or principle is true in all cultures and in all types of creation.

Adam would tend to, cultivate, and dress (Genesis 2:15) The Garden of Eden. I have to believe this taught Adam work ethics, organization, and persistence. Adam needed these important characteristics to be developed before Eve came on the scene.

Which this Garden had a river flowing through so The Garden would be watered. This river divided into four other rivers the name of the first river was Pison which flowed around the land of Havilah where there was gold; the second was named Gihon and this river flowed around the land of Ethiopia; the third river was named Hiddekel which flowed east of Assyria and the fourth was the river Euphrates (Genesis 2:10-14).

Adam was in charge of this massive land God gave it to him and we can correctly say this was his job. What a huge responsibility for Adam to fulfill however God knew Adam was capable and willing to carry out God's Plan.

And some of us have challenges working eight hours in a single building or office. Making excuses that they have too much of a work load. How many of us could have done what Adam did and done it correctly? Hmm? Sounds like to me God will give us whatever it takes to complete the task.

Adam also understood that he was far more superior to that of animals although his needs were the same of animals (food, water, and shelter). God gave Adam choices and his decisions lead him to certain desires, and of course, determined his destiny for his life. Genesis 2:16-17 And The Lord God commanded the man (Adam), saying, Of every tree of the Garden thou mayest freely eat:

But of the tree of the knowledge of good and evil, thou shall not eat of it: for in the day that thou eatest thereof shalt surely die. Help me out here Family, "Why Adam and Eve would be so tempted to a tree that would kill them?" When they had acres upon acres of land to live off of, which gave them the abundant life?

It's something like God giving us fifty businesses bringing in fifty million dollars a month. But this one business, God says, don't touch because it will cause you to have tragedy and lead you to poverty.

Then as time goes by we continue to carry out our normal daily transactions with the fifty businesses and everything is still profitable. Then all of a sudden, offers start coming across the table concerning this one business that God told us not to touch these offers get your attention and they seem attractive and lucrative. So by having the mindset of greed thinking we might be missing out on another good opportunity, and omit the tragedy and poverty God mentioned that we would have by touching this forbidden business.

We begin to deceive ourselves and rationalize by saying, "How can one little business cause me to go under when millions of dollars are already coming consistently?"

Just like the serpent of deception made Adam and Eve believe and say, "How could things go bad when you have so much abundance and you could be missing out on something?"

So ignorantly you take on this business and this business is now in your name. Then shortly thereafter we find that this business is connected to the drug world and all types of wrong doing. Now we are under investigation, then convicted now serving a prison sentence plus eventually the courts find a way to strip us of everything. All because we failed to obey The Voice of The Lord telling us not to engage in that business transaction!

Lesson to be learned never disregard The Voice of God plus disobedience can have a fatal price (Deuteronomy chapter 28). "Is the price worth it?"

Now let's get back into Genesis with God's Creation through Adam.

In today's intelligence I would consider Adam a genius for him to name all the animals, birds, fishes, and insects (Genesis 2:20). This had to take a great deal of time, thought, and revelation.

Because from the name Adam gave these creatures would also determine what kind of behavior or character they would portray throughout their lives of which they had no choice.

A dog has to bark and run on four legs; a bird has to chirp and use their wings to fly; a monkey has to use their arms for climbing and swinging through the trees; and so on with the different traits of the remainder of animals.

When you hear certain animal names you automatically associate that name to a certain animal character or behavior or possibly linked to an animal sound. I understand why some people would take on the study of lions, tigers, reptiles, birds, and sea life as research projects. I also understand this is a career and a lifestyle for some people and is good because they have educated and informed the public from their research.

I've often wondered an animal that is one thousand or two thousand pounds, "What do they eat?" Do you ever hear of these animals that size getting high blood pressure or having a stroke because of their size? I don't think that would be a concern in animal life because, God has designed their body size as part of their survival source. Surely Adam had to learn certain facts about animals and used those facts to give the animals their names.

So by now we see all the preparation being performed for Eve's entrance. But not so much for Eve but for all of mankind, God's Creation, and His Progressive Plan in the earth.

We see a similar preparation for The Church by God operating His Redemptive Plan through His Son Jesus. The Bible refers to The Church as The Body of Christ or His Bride. The preparation Jesus went through to redeem us from the curse of satan and to establish His Church in the earth. Similar on how we should prepare for the coming of our wife.

Ephesians 5:23, 25, 28-29 (AMP) For the husband is head of the wife as Christ is the Head of The Church, Himself the Savior of [His] body.

Husbands, love your wives, as Christ loved The Church and gave Himself up for her,

Even so husbands should love their wives as [being in a sense] their own bodies. He who loves his own wife loves himself.

For no man ever hated his own flesh, but nourishes and carefully protects and cherishes it, as Christ does The Church.

Genesis 2:21-24 (AMP) And The Lord God caused a deep sleep to fall upon Adam; and while he slept, He (God) took one of his (Adam's) ribs or a part of his (Adam's) side and closed up the [place with] flesh.

And the rib or part of his side which The Lord God had taken from the man He (God) built up and made into a woman, and He brought her to the man.

Then Adam said, This [creature] is now bone of my bone and flesh of my flesh; she shall be called Woman, because she was taken out of Man. (*Translated from the womb of a man; wo-man*)

Therefore a man shall leave his father and his mother and shall unite and cleave to his wife, and they shall become one flesh.

Matthew 19:5-6 (AMP) And said, For this reason a man shall leave his father and mother and shall be united firmly (joined inseparably) to his wife, and the two shall become one flesh?

So they are no longer two, but one flesh, What therefore God has joined together, let not man put asunder (separate).

Now Family please allow me to elaborate on the many things that just took place on this Day of Celebration of the beginning of Womanhood.

First, God birthed Woman into the earth unique from any other birth and no other birth came into the earth the same way. God made all of His Living Creation from the dust of the ground. But Woman was designed from an already developed human specimen. That within itself is a miracle for God to make such a Beautiful Creature from a bone. Which, a bone is a replica of a firm structural or strength designed for a certain task.

Song of Solomon 4:4 (AMP) Your neck is like the tower of David, built for an arsenal, (a weapon)… God personally hand crafted her to perfection with every aspect of her being representing a powerful force of beauty, charm, and grace. Song of Solomon 4:7 (AMP) … O my love, how beautiful you are! There is no flaw in you! God placed in Women such intelligence that cannot be matched with any other creature God created.

Proverbs 31:26 (AMP) She opens her mouth in skillful and Godly Wisdom, and on her tongue is the law of kindness [giving counsel and instruction]. Her thoughts and thinking process is so rapid and advance only she can reveal or send many messages with just one motion or one look without speaking a word.

I'm convinced the true definition of progressive thinking is a Woman. A Woman's femininity cannot be duplicated nor is there a script to be followed. Her moves are delicate and smooth as we see another side of her that can only be defined as beauty.

Women's steps are planted for a precise direction flowing in glamour and musical silence. Her eyes are piercing with firm confidence, strength, and gentleness. A Women's touch is filled with motivation, tenderness, with extreme and strict attentiveness. Her fragrance is above that of any flower that weighs heavy and lingers in any atmosphere. Putting all that together and we have a Complete and Human Elegance perfect with silent poetry which sends a loud message saying, "I'm Woman, I'm here!"

God put this Woman together and presented her to Adam bone of your bone flesh of your flesh. God expressed that Adam you don't have to be alone anymore She (Woman) is perfect "for your help meet." Genesis 2:18

When Adam announced that Eve is bone of his bone and flesh of his flesh this is when the marriage of Adam and Eve took place, which was the first marriage of mankind between Man and Woman.

There is a valuable lesson to be learned here before Woman came on the scene. Everything was in place nothing was missing or broken. Total satisfaction and completion was the only order of the day.

I see God placing high priorities on what a Woman is to experience when we as men are to take her on as our wife.

First and foremost we men are to be born again believers and have a strong relationship with our Father God. If you haven't given your life to Jesus as your personal Savior now would be a good time to repeat out loud Romans 10:9 I confess with my mouth the Lord Jesus and I believe in my heart that God raised Him from the dead... (AMP) Romans 10:9 Because if you acknowledge and confess with your lips that Jesus is Lord and in your heart believe (adhere to, trust in, and rely on the Truth) that God raised Him from the dead, you will be saved.

It's just that simple God doesn't want to make this hard or difficult. Just by repeating Romans 10:9 and seriously mean it then you have just been birthed into the Body of Christ. Congratulations! You have just made the most important decision you can make.

You may be saying what do I do now? You need to find a Church where the true teaching of God's Word is being taught. Sitting under a true Man or Woman of God will make a big difference in determining your growth and maturity with your new found life.

In your study time you may want to start reading the first four books of the New Testament: Matthew, Mark, Luke, and John. These books show how Jesus taught His Disciples and multitudes of people The Principles of Godly Living, the attitude we must have when living Godly, and the benefit we will experience once we allow these Godly Principles to take effect in our lives on a daily basis.

As you read in the books Matthew, Mark, Luke, and John you'll see the attitude of Christ and the passion He has for people. How He performed miracles of healing, deliverances, and provisions.

These readings may carry you to other areas of The Bible in giving more Truth about who you are and what you can do. Your faith will increase with every revelation or new found knowledge and you will start believing that you are what you are reading. This is what believers do so I say to this new believer, "Don't stop this process that can take place in your life!"

This process of the new birth is the only way a new purpose and a new defined direction will start and that God has specifically designed for you. As we see who we are in God's Word and practice these principles daily. Doors will begin to open following with Godly opportunities which will lead us down a path that's filled with prosperity and wealth.

As we travel in Godly ways our thinking will line-up with God's Word. Our desires will be in line with God's desires; our thoughts will be in line with God's thoughts; our steps will be and remain in God's Path.

Matthew 6:33 (AMP) But seek (aim at and strive after) first of all His Kingdom and His Righteousness (His way of doing and being right), and all these things taken together will be given you besides. Most times this will divert us from our own agendas which is nothing wrong with having plans however it states in Proverbs 3:6 (AMP) In all your ways know, recognize, and acknowledge Him, (God) and He will direct and make straight and plain your paths. As we do this then operating in the ways of Ephesians fifth chapter will not be a problem.

Just like God provided in abundance for Adam which led up to the marriage of Eve because Adam was obedient with his personal relationship with God. God will also provide us with lasting commodities necessary to start a harmonious marriage. And if some are already married these things can still happen.

So what necessary commodities are you talking about? For starters job/careers, house, and transportation all these built a security safe net for a wife.

She likes to know if there is going to be a steady flow of income covering all expenses including nails, hair do's, shopping, and occasional restaurant entrees. This thought may be going through her mind, "Can I live in a house that can be our own without sharing it with relatives or other apartment tenants?" There can never be too much privacy.

She will want to know, "Do we have a reliable vehicle(s) where weekly repairs are not a concern?" How much debt do I (The Man) have and is it a good decision to carry this debt into the marriage when it's been a statistical fact that most marriages end because of small amounts of finances? If I'm out of debt before marriage then after marriage it will be a lot easier to work on her debt. But two debts with living and other expenses is a definite hardship on the marriage.

By having all this in order, and it's highly possible, just look at how God provided for Adam. God has no problem providing abundance for us to be able to shower our wives with and to treat our wife like The Precious Jewel that she is. In 1Peter 2:9 states, that we are of a "Royal Priesthood" which is just superior thinking through God's Word and applying that thinking in our lives.

We are Kings and Queens in this earth although we are commanded to obey authority. We can not be good leaders if we are not good followers. By understanding that revelation now we can begin to ravish our wives with the royalty, comfort, and the pleasures that A Godly Man has to offer which I feel is our basic responsibility for God's Most Beautiful Creation.

How a Woman Utilizes Her Godly Qualities –

As I mention previously A Woman has not a script to follow nor can anything about her be duplicated.

This also is true for a Godly Woman however A Godly Woman brings more to table in the way of opportunities, ideas, and options through her "Anointing."

A Godly Woman knows how to tap into God's resources by allowing God's Anointing to flow through her on a consistent basis.

She realizes that a closed door is not the final result but she seeks out to find the key and gracefully walks through that door of unlimited opportunities.

As a Single Woman she stands equipped and qualified to make adjustments where needed. Others may doubt her or give her destructive criticism but she turns that into a positive force and uses that as fuel to complete the task.

She always counts up the cost and determined what steps she needs to take. When accomplishments or completion arises her joy is the highlight of the hour and contagious to everyone involved.

A woman's endurance levels are superior to any other because God can speak through a three year child and make it plain if He so chooses. What I've found with A Woman, she will explain a thing from A-Z not excluding any detail.

On other hand, we as Men will use the shortest route possible to get to a certain destination. On many occasions I've been guilty of that very technique which sometimes I have to go back and pull the pieces together so understanding is clearer.

However, not many times will you find A Woman back tracking, because she has already prepared explanations and definitions to perfection.

So, when she gets married she is accustomed to taking her qualities to unlimited levels. And when her husband is A Man of God carrying and living out The Plan of God for his life he is anointed to enhance what she has already. And not become intimidated over her qualities although realizing there is a place in their marriage where she can be just as fruitful as him.

If the husband is secure within himself and his relationship with God negativity or inferiority has no room to reside. Because the Plan that God has for his life has also been tailored made for their marriage and children and will fit into every step that the two of them make.

As children enter into the picture challenges with their children will be at a minimal because by the parents being of one flesh they speak the same thing and the children only hear one voice.

Discipline will set in a lot sooner because this child is first rooted in stability. This allows more of a healthy lifestyle for the child because of Godly Principles flowing through their life consistently. The child is more confident and will not be afraid to take on challenges which will allow them to excel beyond their peers.

Someone might be saying, "What does that have to do with Woman's Qualities?" By understanding the growth process in the home and with children now the husband has A Godly Plan for the Family.

As this Plan has been proven to work for the husband and the wife before the children arrived now, the wife implements this Plan into the children and they start to see more of a harvest of God's Results through His Plan. She finds different ways to get the children to receive this learning but fun concept and most times the parents will find a way to make learning fun.

For most this Godly Process may be in full operation with outstanding results. Now our Families are strong with daily progress this leads to us having a strong Church with daily progress.

To sum it all up at this point; A Woman is like a Monument which requires strategic foundations. Her awesome structure is massive in beauty, wit, charm, and desire all of which are qualities of Queens and this demands respect and honor from all of God's Creation. Because of Her Royalty now she produces flawless Glamour a proven definition of perfection "Our Women!"

Printed in the United States
By Bookmasters